Collec...
Development
Policies
for College Libraries

CLIP Note #11

Collection Development Policies

for College Libraries

CLIP Note #11

Compiled by
Theresa Taborsky, *Director,*
and **Patricia Lenkowski,** *Reference Librarian*
with the assistance of
Anne Webb and Lisa Lewis
Wolfgram Memorial Library
Widener University

College Library Information Packet Committee
College Libraries Section
Association of College and Research Libraries
A Division of the American Library Association

Published by the Association of College and Research Libraries
A Division of the American Library Association
50 East Huron Street
Chicago, IL 60611-7295

ISBN: 0-8389-7295-0

The paper used in this publication meets the minumum requirements of American National Standard for Information Sciences—
Permanence of Paper for Printed Library Materials, ANSI Z39.48-1984. ∞

TABLE OF CONTENTS

INTRODUCTION

Objective

The College Library Information Packet (CLIP) Notes program provides "college and small university libraries with state-of-the-art reviews and current documentation of library practices and procedures of relevance to them." This CLIP Note is re-examining the issue dealt with by one of the pilot studies, CLIP Note #2, published in 1981. The intervening years have brought numerous changes to the environment faced by academic libraries, including declining budgets, new academic programs, automation and networking for resource sharing. These changes, which have affected both collection development and the acquisition of library materials, should be reflected in current Collection Development Policies. Recent and growing interest of college librarians in collection development issues, as reflected in the literature and in numerous conferences, workshops and discussion groups, has presumably resulted in more formalized collection development guidelines or revision of obsolete ones. The search for evidence to document these assumptions resulted in Clip Note #11.

Document Gathering

In March 1988 a questionnaire was mailed to a select list of librarians and administrators of small and medium-sized academic libraries. The base for the list was the Carnegie Foundation's classification of institutions of higher education. These librarians had expressed to the CLIP Notes Committee their willingness to participate in such surveys and have contributed to previous studies. Their number (193) is a non-stratified, non-random sampling of the college library universe. One hundred seven responded and of these, sixty-two indicated that they have a written Collection Development Policy.

Analysis of the Survey Results

The sample questionnaire and the summary of the responses are included. Due to the nature of the topic, it would not be useful to reduce the figures to strict numbers of averages and extremes. It might be left to the reader to interpret questions and answers as trends and/or to compare them to one's own experience and perception.

The rather high rate of return (55.4%) confirms the premise that there is considerable interest in this topic. There seems to be no pattern suggesting that library size has any bearing on the existence of a Collection Development Policy document. Nor is there a visible connection between library and/or materials budget size and the policy. The majority of the documents submitted are recent or recently revised. Interestingly, more than half of them were written by or with the active participation of the Library Director. Fewer were the product of committee work than that of an individual. The great majority of the policies utilized resources published in library literature and also samples from other institutions. For some there was ample input from teaching faculty, though still only in the minority of libraries. Only three used outside consultants. Many of the answers suggested that the responsibility for collection development belongs primarily to the librarians, both from a philosophical perspective as well as in practice. Most of the comments were reproduced with the survey results, eliminating some redundancy. Many suggest issues of interest to those surveyed which were not addressed or

1

answered by us, for example, the use of allocation formulas, approval plans, joint collection development policies within cooperatives, faculty's role and impact in collection building, rationale for major commitments like indexes, abstracts, and CD-ROM databases. Perhaps they will be developed into topics for future inquiries.

The Nature and Variety of Collection Development Policies

The documents submitted show diversity in content, format, and amount of detail, though more prominent were the similarities. Those which deal with a complete range of acquisition issues usually include mission statements or the reason for writing a policy. The organization usually addresses different formats of library material and often, but not always, describes collection needs in various academic subjects. The latter frequently quantifies desirable collection levels following the library conspectus of RLG or similar definitions for the intensity of collecting in specific areas.

The scope of the documents ranges from a couple of pages of a quasi "mission statement" to the minute description of procedures to be followed by library staff as well as by faculty submitting requests for purchase. Some are indeed part of library-faculty handbooks or acquisition department manuals. Evidently, it is difficult to separate policy from procedure, substance from format. One can also see how important it is to establish a means to implement collection development guidelines. It might be interesting to note that although this was not the objective of the survey, many allocation formulas were sent to us, either part of a Collection Development Policy or as a separate self-contained document. The use of allocation formulas are somewhat controversial and may deserve a separate study.

Selection of Documents

The policies reproduced in this CLIP Note were selected to illustrate the variety of approaches to collection development in use today. Several documents are included in their entirety due to their thorough coverage of the topic. Excerpts from complete policies are included because of their uniqueness.

WORKS CITED

Morein, P. Grady. "What is a CLIP Note?" College and Research Libraries News 46 (1985): 226.

CLIP Note SURVEY (RESULTS)

SUMMARY OF THE CLIP Notes SURVEY
Collection Development Policy Statements
In College Libraries

GENERAL INFORMATION (to be kept confidential)

Name of Respondent _____

Title _____

Institution Name _____

Address _____

_____

A. LIBRARY PROFILE   (Figures are for Fiscal Year 1987-88 unless otherwise noted.)

1. Number of full-time equivalent (FTE) students:
   98 responses; Range 347-9606; Mean 2471.7; Median 2105

2. Number of full-time equivalent librarians
   102 responses; Range 1-39; Mean 8.53; Median 7.0

3. Total library budget (check one):   107 responses
   less than $200,000 ___4___
   $200,001-$500,000 ___20___
   $500,001-$1,000,000 ___43___
   $1,000,000-$2,000,000 _36___
   over $2,000,000 ___4___

4. Total materials budget (check one)   107 responses
   less than $50,000 ___2___
   $50,001-$100,000 ___6___
   $100,000-$200,000 ___28___
   $200,000-$300,000 ___24___
   over $300,000 ___47___

5. Number of volumes in the library:
   105 responses; Range 57,000-1,479,652; Mean 318,631.4; Median 238,600

6. Average number of volumes added per year:
   103 responses; Range 1000-40,000; Mean 7638.8; Median 6,000

5

B. COLLECTION DEVELOPMENT POLICY

1. Do you have a written Collection Development
   Policy (CDP)?   107 responses

   yes _62_ No _45_   If no skip to C5.

   Comments: We began this process in 1982 and did some of the preparation
   but the results were never compiled into a policy or statement. Informal
   guidelines did result in some areas the work was done by librarians serving
   as liaisons to academic departments.

   Just general guidelines, not a total policy. Since it's only a guideline,
   no approval needed. One or two departments have constructed a real
   collection development policy document...of great use.

2. If your answer is _yes_, please send a copy of such documentation,
   complete or partial, even if it covers only special subjects and/or
   formats (e.g. rare book collection, audiovisuals, etc.)
                                                     46 responses

3. When was the policy written?   62 responses
                        13 written between 1969-1978
                        20 written between 1979-1984
                        29 written between 1985-1988

   Has it been revised? yes _22_ no _40_
   How often: _6_ yearly
                  _6_ every 3 years
                  _1_ every 5 years
                  _9_ other -occasionally or partially, as needed

4. Who wrote the CDP? (check all that apply)   61 responses

            _35_ library director
            _32_ acquisitions/collection development librarian
            _24_ library committee
            _4_ faculty committee
            _17_ other -e.g. head of reference, various groups of
                 librarians, faculty input, subject specialists

5. Indicate the resources used in creating a CDP: 58 responses
   (check all that apply)

   _48_ published library literature
   _16_ classification schedules
   _48_ sample policies from other libraries
   _3_ consultants
   _29_ input from teaching faculty
   _12_ other-e.g. experience, mission statement, goals and objectives
        of academic administration, approval plan profile,
        codification of existing practices

6. Who approved and adopted the CDP? (check all that apply)   59 responses

   _51_ library director
   _18_ academic administration
   _20_ teaching faculty
   _28_ library faculty
   _11_ other -e.g. consortium directors, library faculty committees,
        students (!)

C. USE AND USEFULNESS OF CDP

   1. Who is responsible for its implementation and revision: 61 responses
      (check all that apply)

      _38_ acquisitions/collection development librarian
      _40_ library administration
      _17_ library committee
      _4_ faculty committee
      _9_ other -e.g. all librarians, tri-college task force, liaison
          librarians, academic departments

7

2. Does it include policies to select: 58 responses
   (check all that apply)

   _58_ books
   _52_ periodicals
   _23_ standing orders
   _42_ AV material
   _22_ computer software
   _10_ approval plans
   _14_ other formats (specify) -e.g. almost all formats, sound
       recordings, scores, maps, dissertations, textbooks, microform,
       archival materials

3. Does this policy address the issue of cooperative purchasing with other
   libraries?   yes _12_   no _46_   58 responses

   Comments: No, but we do cooperative buying.
   Not directly but it assumes it will occur.

4. How important is it, in your opinion, to develop further guidelines
   for: 59 responses

	Not at all				Very important
a. books	15	8	13	10	12
b. periodicals	10	5	15	16	13
c. computer software	8	8	15	10	16
d. AV materials	8	7	15	14	3
e. electronic reference tools	3	4	10	17	19

5. How important, in your opinion, is it to have a written collection
   development policy?   100 responses

Not important				Very important
3	3	24	33	37

8

5. Please explain briefly what a CDP can provide for your library.

Selected responses:

Documentation of existing policies - standardization.

Very little since the faculty does upwards of 70% of book selection.

A plan for growth.

...use against over zealous faculty.

...a detailed and well thought out CDP...I'd hate to see it get inflexible.

...a CDP [is] a requirement in a research university, not...in a liberal arts setting.

Consensus between the Library and the teaching staff...

...a mechanism for educating and communicating with the faculty and the college administration...

The same for any library: a raison d'etre for library purchases in any format.

It...points out weaknesses...where we need resource-sharing.

...departmental profiles...are less rigid than CDPs.

Guidance to Collection Development Officers, Faculty/Library Liaison Officers, and others involved in the day-to-day process of selecting materials. Provide information to University administration and faculty committees. Serve as a guideline for long range planning. Provide information for inter-library cooperative collection development.

...comprehensive statement of collecting needs and interests to (1) faculty and students (2) library staff (3) other libraries for resource sharing purposes.

If...there is no possibility of special collection development projects, usefulness of CDP is questionable.

Since we do not allocate materials budget by % to departments we need...to explain...particularly to outside evaluators.

The process of writing the document may be more important than the finished piece of paper.

...standards to use in analyzing the support [of] the university's curricular and research needs.

"Protection".

Assistance in budget allocation...in justifying acquisitions.

Our own CDP guides wise use of funds in a time of tight budgets and high book costs. Departmental policies help...to build specific areas......The Tri-College policy is saving each library significant sums through reduction of needless duplication.

Direction and guidance, pure and simple.

...insure relevancy of acquisitions to the curriculum...basis for acceptance/-rejection of gift materials...for rejecting arcane/esoteric requests.

Justification for budget allocations.

Irrefutable backup for decisions.

Guidelines for budget allocations...for cooperative collection.

Some limitation on faculty buying expensive, unused materials. Faculty...have had almost total control of collection development, and they have done a mediocre job at best in most disciplines.

A CDP can provide...an understanding of the nature of the collection.

Approved authority to support decisions which might conflict with faculty requests. Control over the collection building process.

By making decisions ahead of time as to what the library should be selecting, individual decisions about particular items are made much simpler.

Prevent arbitrary purchases...coordinate...curriculum...with supportive library materials.

Gives purposeful, systematic, and institution-oriented direction to selection activity. The process of putting it together is also of great value.

The CDP is a blueprint for the future library growth. It ties together instructional objectives, budgetary expenditures and the creation of a balanced library collection.

All librarians participate in collection development, serving as liaisons to several departments. It's important that they all understand and operate under the same policies.

Guide faculty. Make funds more effective in serving the needs of students.

6. To what extent has interest in a strong in-house collection changed in your library in recent years? 98 responses

	decreased greatly	decreased somewhat	same	increased somewhat	increased greatly
librarians	2	6	39	29	22
faculty	1	6	41	37	12
college administration	6	7	48	24	13
library administration	4	6	39	21	28

10

D. SELECTION PROCESS

1. The following individuals or groups make recommendations: 105 responses
(check all that apply)

    105 teaching faculty

    105 librarians (and other library staff)

    81 students

    Comments: Limited...suggestions are welcome...seldom
    do...minimal...non academic, occasionally...they are not
    excluded, it is simply rare to get a request from a student.

    30 other -e.g. staff, administrators, community members, outside
    borrowers

2. The following groups or individuals approve or disapprove the purchase
of titles recommended: (check all that apply)   104 responses

    71 acquisitions/collection development librarian

    38 subject specialist librarian/bibliographer

    8 library committee

    10 faculty committee

    65 library administration

    Comments: in unusual instances only; occasionally.

    20 other -e.g. academic department head; director of libraries
    and department chair; purchasing office and dean of faculty;
    academic department chairs approve requests charged to their
    departmental accounts; serials librarian for serial standing
    orders; departmental liaisons, from approved allocations;
    director of libraries; academic departmental library
    representatives or chairs

3. Decisions are based on: (check all that apply)   105 responses

   _70_ collection development guidelines
   _85_ subject expertise
   _86_ subjective individual judgement
   _35_ consensus based on group review
        Comments: especially for periodicals; [for] very high cost
        items.
   _17_ other _e.g. faculty recommendation; critical reviews;
        appropriateness to the curriculum; availability of funds;
        recommended lists; demands of students._

4. Do you use an allocation formula in budgeting for library purchases?
   yes _43_   no _59_   102 responses

   If yes, please attach a copy to the questionnaire.   22 received

        Comments: availability + cost + # majors + # faculty + # courses
        i.e.   a + c + m + f + courses * budget/s = allocation, then
        allowances made for new programs, prior spending patterns, etc.

        No, though for years we have used the multiple variables any
        formula might include but in a soft way rather than as a hard
        formula.

        Headcount: 35% faculty; 35% graduate student; 30% undergraduate.

        Basically same as Scudder, Mary C. "Using Choice in an Allocation
        Formula in a Small Academic Library." Choice June 1987, 1506ff.

        Yes but only in a very limited way.   We are trying to move to an
        approval plan.

        Formula: Circulation by "dept." Dewey nos. [x2], no. of students,
        no. of majors, and cost of materials order last year.

        It's a parameter guess rather than formula.

        Not strictly a budget but rather guidelines for library staff.

12

E. LIBRARY MANAGEMENT

1. There are other aspects of library management which may need written guidelines. Please indicate your priorities for written policies by ranking the following services (number 1 is most important and 7 is least important):   81 responses

	1	2	3	4	5	6	7
collection development	54	10	3	5	5	4	0
reference services	13	13	18	14	15	4	2
bibliographic instruction	2	12	13	17	14	16	1
new technologies	0	8	14	10	18	22	3
res. sharing with other lib.	10	13	12	18	15	8	1
audiovisual services	3	16	1	12	9	19	1
other	3	4	1	1	1	1	5

other   e.g. circulation services, database searches; personnel policies/staff management; outside user access

2. Does your library have any stated policies for developing services to access resources outside your library?
   (check all that apply)   87 responses
   _81_ interlibrary loan

   _54_ consortia

   _50_ formal resource sharing arrangements with other libraries

   _36_ union catalogs

   _34_ delivery service

   _29_ networking (communications)

   _7_ other e.g. joint library automation and resource sharing project with [other] colleges; informal arrangements with community librarians; services to outside researchers

   IF YOU HAVE ANY DOCUMENTED POLICY PLEASE SEND US A COPY.
                                                            12 received

3. How much is resource sharing affecting your traditional purchasing pattern?   108 responses

   Not at all   Very much
       21   30   41   9   7

13

4. Is Interlibrary loan increasing/decreasing?   106 responses

	Decreasing		Same		Increasing
a. borrowing	0	3	14	48	41
b. lending	1	2	12	45	44

5. Do online and/or other electronic databases influence your selections for purchase (e.g. citations for materials not in your collection)?

                                                               99 responses

	Not at all				Very much
for books	21	34	22	18	4
for periodicals	16	28	21	24	10

6. In which way does your state (region) encourage resource sharing? (Check all that apply)   102 responses

_59_ grants or other subsidies

_68_ formal networking arrangements

  Comments: under development; perennially under discussion.

_54_ promoting new technologies

_66_ workshops

_67_ union catalog

  Comments: Periodicals; serials, newspapers

_61_ delivery service

_46_ telecommunications

  Comments: electronic mail, telefax

_5_ not at all

_3_ other   most initiatives taken by individual libraries or small consortia; central circulation/online catalog system

Comments: Resource sharing is primarily among the five academic libraries. The state does not play a major role.

F. SUMMARY

1. Did you participate in the 1981 survey for CLIP Study #2 on Collection Development Policy?   72 responses

   yes _16_   no _56_

COLLECTION DEVELOPMENT POLICIES

COMPLETE DOCUMENTS

DRAFT

COLLECTION DEVELOPMENT POLICY STATEMENT FOR
GINGRICH LIBRARY, ALBRIGHT COLLEGE
READING, PENNSYLVANIA

March 1988

COLLECTION DEVELOPMENT POLICY STATEMENT FOR GINGRICH LIBRARY, ALBRIGHT COLLEGE

I.   INTRODUCTION

This policy is proposed as a statement of the operating guidelines used by the Gingrich Library in its acquisition and maintenance of materials. Rising costs, increases in publishing output, and relentlessly increasing demands for information resources necessitate careful materials selection, soundly based on an understanding of the immediate and future goals of the library and the institution and students it serves. A collection must be systematically shaped and developed in order to make best use of the funds allotted it. The following are general policies which guide the process of developing Gingrich Library's collection.

In this policy, the word "materials" shall be used to encompass all classes of materials which a library collects and makes available to its users.

II.   OBJECTIVES

The primary goal of the Gingrich Library is the support of the undergraduate academic programs at Albright College. Institutional objectives, as stated in the college catalog, include
A. Offering a general studies program which provides a liberal education to all students, and
B. Providing undergraduate programs in the arts, humanities, social and natural sciences, and professional programs.
With the addition of adjunct graduate programs offered on the campus, the Library assumes collection development responsibilities in those graduate areas as a secondary goal.

III.   SELECTION RESPONSIBILITY

Ultimate responsibility for the development and maintenance of the library's collection rests with the Library Director, who has delegated this responsibility to the Collection Development Librarian. All requests for materials are reviewed for their adherence to the selection guidelines (as stated in Section V. SELECTION GUIDELINES), and must be approved by the Collection Development Librarian. It is the Library Director's responsibility to assign selection responsibilities to library staff and to solicit selections from faculty in their respective areas of expertise (through the mechanism of a faculty allotment of library funds). It is hoped that faculty continually monitor their professional literature for appropriate library acquisitions, and that they make the library staff aware of library material most useful for course requirements and for students' research needs. Student and staff requests for acquisition of materials are also welcomed and encouraged, and are reviewed by the same standards as are requests from all other sources.

IV.   FUND ALLOCATION

It is the Library Director's responsibility to allocate the materials budget in such a way as to fulfill the library's collection development goals. The library's materials budget is currently divided about equally between serials and monographs. The funds available for monographs are divided between the thirty nine subject and format lines (see APPENDIX 1: SUBJECT LINES). The amount allocated to each subject area is built upon the collection development formula which reflects such factors as the number of courses taught in the subject area, the number of students and faculty involved, and the average cost of materials in the field (see APPENDIX 2: ALLOCATION FORMULA). All subject areas will receive a minimum allotment based upon the number of faculty teaching in those areas.

18

Albright College
Lancaster, Pennsylvania

The basic mathematical model will be used in arriving at the allocations, with the realization that some flexibility is necessary for changing conditions (for example, new course offerings, new levels of academic accreditation for programs, changes in student research requirements, etc.). Unless there are major changes, the budget allocation will be revised biennially and appropriate changes will be made.

V. SELECTION GUIDELINES

The institutional goals which are stated in Section II must always provide the framework for selection. Thus the major responsibility and top priority of the library lies with the teaching programs at the undergraduate level. The library endeavors to serve the needs of the faculty either by purchasing (if the materials can also be used by the student body) or by securing through interlibrary loan those resources needed for faculty study and research. Although at a much lower priority, the library services the entire college community through the purchase of recreational, cultural and general information materials.

The quality of content and fulfillment of academic curricular need are the first criteria against which any potential item is evaluated. Specific considerations in choosing individual items include some or all of the following:

● lasting value of the content
● appropriateness of level of treatment
● strength of present holdings in same or similar subject area
● cost
● suitability of format to content
● authoritativeness of the author or reputation of publisher

Other guidelines are also enforced:

1) Textbooks are not normally purchased. The exceptions are those which have earned reputation as "classics" in their fields, or when a textbook is the only or best sources of information on a particular topic.

2) Duplicates are purchased only under unusual circumstances.

3) In instances where the cost of an item is high and the demand is low, the holdings of nearby libraries are considered in determining whether or not an order should be made.

4) When there is an option of paper or hardcopy, the choice is based on expected use, lasting value of content, and cost differential.

5) Lost or stolen materials shall be replaced after 6-9 months (or immediately, if needed) if they are available. The current book trade and aforementioned selection criteria shall be considered.

6) Except for foreign language dictionaries, the library acquires primarily English language reference and research sources. Literature and language materials that are used heavily in the teaching or learning of foreign languages are collected as well.

7) The majority of selections are current publications. The library recognizes the need for retrospective purchases, and systematically uses standard bibliographies and other evaluation tools to locate and fill gaps in the collection. However, in view of the difficulty and expense in obtaining out-of-print and reprinted material, it is most important to spend funds for valuable current publications of long-term worth, thus preventing a future need for retrospective buying.

The library staff uses the following as primary selection tools, with additional sources as needed: *Choice* (monthly), *Library Journal* (bi-weekly), *American Libraries* (monthly), *New York Review of Books* (bi-weekly), *New York Times Book Review* (weekly), *Booklist* (bi-monthly), *Publishers Weekly* (weekly), publishers' catalogs and pre-publication literature, selected subject-specific professional journals, *Guide to Reference Books*, *American Reference Books Annual*, and *Books for College Libraries*.

19

VI. SERIALS

Because serials represent an ongoing commitment, budgeting and selection differ from that involved in purchasing monographs. Because each periodical title does involve a prospective longstanding commitment, and because of increasing periodical subscription rates and limited funds, acquisition of a serial title requires, and receives, substantially more consideration than acquisition of a single monograph. Gingrich Library presently subscribes to about 1000 serial titles, including serials, periodicals, newspapers and indexing services. A serials review committee, composed of the collection development staff, meets regularly for the purpose of reviewing existing commitments and considering requests for major new subscriptions. Users requesting addition of new periodical titles are asked to complete a form describing the value of the title to the library's collection (see APPENDIX 3: SERIAL REQUEST FORM). Back runs of qualifying serials or journal subscriptions are purchased only as deemed necessary or as the budget permits.

Some or all of the following criteria are used in evaluating titles for acquisition or cancellation:

- support of present academic curriculum
- strength of the existing collection
- present use of this or other periodicals in this subject area
- projected future use
- cost, projected availability of funds
- reputation of journal and/or inclusion in a prominent abstracting and indexing source
- if not owned, number of recent interlibrary loan requests for this periodical

VII. NON-PRINT MATERIAL

Requests for non-print materials (audio and video cassettes, slides, etc.) are evaluated on the same basis as are monographs, with special emphasis on the suitability of the format to the content, and on the quality of the production. Non-print materials are considered simply a different format of subject information. Evaluation, weeding and replacement of non-print items follow the same guidelines and procedures as for monographs, with one exception. Since non-print materials are used more often for classroom display, all items must be previewed by the faculty member or their delegate to insure the usability of the materials.

VIII. SPECIALTY COLLECTIONS

Most materials that are obtained, including government documents, are integrated into the general collection. The three major exceptions are described below.

A. Library Collection (LC)

The Library Collection is a small, frequently replenished group of popular or best selling books. This collection is minimally cataloged and is intended for recreational reading. Once the items are no longer used, they are re-evaluated and some of the materials are added to the general collection.

B. Special Collections

The library maintains two types of special collections that are segregated from the rest of the collection in locked areas. The first group are the archival collections of Albrightiana and the EUB (Evangelical United Brethren). The second group are the subject and gift collections, e.g., Dick, Nolan Room, and Rare Books.

C. Chemistry Library

The library maintains one branch library in the science building to contain materials used by the Chemistry students. These materials include *recent years of Chemical Abstracts*, most of the recent chemistry journals and serials, and most of the current chemistry books that are catalogued by the Library of Congress in the 540s, and some of those catalogued in the 660s and 564s.

IX. GIFTS

Gifts are encouraged, with the understanding that the library may dispose of them or add them to the collection at its discretion, and in the same manner as purchased material. As a general rule, gift books will be added based on the same criteria as purchased ones. The Library assumes no responsibility for appraisal of gift items (see APPENDIX 4: STATEMENT ON APPRAISAL OF GIFTS), nor can the Library accept gifts under restricted conditions.

X. COLLECTION MAINTENANCE AND EVALUATION

Weeding is an important aspect of collection development in the college library. Upon arrival of new editions, the reference staff evaluates previous editions and withdraws those deemed outdated. The reference collection is continually monitored for outdated material, which is replaced or withdrawn. Individual sections of the general collection are periodically reviewed. Faculty are encouraged to assist in spotting outdated or inaccurate materials in their areas of expertise.

XI. COOPERATIVE NETWORKS

With advances in automation and participation in library networks (Associated College Libraries of Central Pennsylvania, OCLC, PALINET, and the Berks Country Library Association), the decisions made by the Gingrich Library become more significant to those involved in collection development. As it becomes increasingly apparent that no college library can provide all of the materials needed by its users, it becomes extremely advantageous to share resources. Thus, each advance in automation has led to increasing interlibrary loan activities. New breakthroughs in online catalogs that extend beyond the individual library make cooperative collection development more of an alternative for the Gingrich Library than has been possible or feasible in the past. Future revisions of this policy statement will undoubtedly reflect mutual reliance for specific subject resources.

XII. INTELLECTUAL FREEDOM

The Gingrich Library of Albright College supports the American Library Association's BILL OF RIGHTS, its INTELLECTUAL FREEDOM STATEMENT, and its statement on CHALLENGED MATERIALS. The Library attempts to purchase materials which represent differing opinions on controversial matters. Selection is without partisanship regarding matters of race, sex, religion or moral philosophy.

APPENDIX 1: SUBJECT AREAS

ACC	Accounting
ART	Art
AV	Audiovisual Materials
BIO	Biology
BUS	Business
CHE	Chemistry
CLA	Classical Languages
CLO	Clothing & Textiles, Fashion Design
CSC	Computer & Information Science
DEP	Depository Accounts with the Federal Government
ECO	Economics
EDU	Education
ENG	English Language & Literature, Composition, Communications
FRE	French Language & Literature
GEN	General Information
GER	German Language & Literature
GLH	Genealogy & Local History
HIS	History
LIB	Library Science
LIT	Non-English Lit in the English Language (not appropriate for other areas)
LRC	Library Collection (LC)
MAT	Math
MBA	Masters in Business Administration
MFL	Non-English Lit in Native Language (not appropriate for other categories)
MHA	Masters in Health Administration
MUS	Music
NUR	Nursing
NUT	Nutrition
PED	Physical Education
PHI	Philosophy
PHY	Physics
POS	Political Science
PSY	Psychology
REC	Records
REF	Reference Works
REL	Religion
SOC	Sociology & Social Welfare
SPA	Spanish Language & Literature
WST	Women's Studies

Albright College
Reading, Pennsylvania

APPENDIX 2: ALLOCATION FORMULA

$$\frac{A + B + C + D}{4} = \text{Factor \% of Budget}$$

A = % of faculty in Department

B = % of courses given by Department

C = % of students serviced by Department

D = % cost of books by subject areas

(It is understood that each subject area will receive a minimum allotment based on the number of faculty teaching in that area.)

Albright College
Reading, Pennsylvania

APPENDIX 3: SERIAL REQUEST FORM

Title: _____

Frequency _____ Price _____ Beginning date _____

Since limited funds and the need to maintain a balanced collection require that we add titles selectively, we would appreciate answers to the following questions:

How did you become aware of this publication? _____
_____

Why is it important to the Albright library collection? _____
_____

How do you plan to use this publication for your classes? (e.g., assigned readings, term papers, library projects that require use, supplementary source of information, students asked to look at copies, etc.) _____
_____

Please assign a rating (check one):

_____ Absolutely essential (even if other titles in this field will have to be cancelled)
_____ Required to keep our collection adequate
_____ Would add strength to our collection
_____ Welcome if funds were available

Your name: _____

Department: _____

Phone number or extension: _____

Do you wish to be notified if this title is acquired?
_____ Yes _____ No

Thank you for your interest.

_____

Bibliographic verification--Staff use

Ulrich's _____ ed. _____ page $_____ price
        Indexed in:

Reviews located:

Issue previewed:

24

APPENDIX 4: STATEMENT ON APPRAISAL OF GIFTS

Developed by the Committee on Manuscript Collections of the Rare Books and Manuscripts Section. Approved by the Association of College & Research Libraries Board of Directors on February 1, 1973, in Washington D.C.

1. The appraisal of a gift to a library for tax purposes generally is the responsibility of the donor since it is the donor who benefits from the tax deduction. Generally, the cost of appraisal should be borne by the donor.

2. The library should at all times protect the interests of its donors as best it can and should suggest the desirability of appraisals whenever such a suggestion would be in order.

3. To protect both its donors and itself, the library as an interested party, ordinarily should not appraise gifts made to it. It is recognized, however, that on occasion the library may wish to appraise small gifts, since many of them are not worth the time and expense an outside appraisal requires. Generally, however, the library will limit its assistance to the donor to:
   a. providing him with information such as auction records and dealer's catalogs;
   b. suggestions of appropriate professional appraisers who might be consulted;
   c. administrative and processing services which might assist the appraiser in making an accurate evaluation.

4. The acceptance of a gift which has been appraised by a third, and disinterested party, does not in any way imply an endorsement of the appraisal by the library.

5. An archivist, curator, or librarian, if he is conscious that as an expert he may have to prove his competence in court, may properly act as an independent appraiser of library materials. He should not in any way suggest that his appraisal is endorsed by his library (such as by the use of the library's letterhead), nor should he ordinarily act in this fashion (except when handling small gifts) if his institution is to receive the donation.

IRWIN LIBRARY SYSTEM
Of
BUTLER UNIVERSITY

COLLECTION DEVELOPMENT POLICY

Butler University
Indianapolis, Indiana

Preface

This document provides an overall plan and specific guidelines for the development of the collections of the library. It seeks to make the best possible use of the resources currently available to meet the instructional and research needs of Butler students and faculty.

The policy will also serve as a guide for collection analysis. Levels of collecting have been established for every subject area identified by the Library of Congress classification system. The levels of collecting used are national standards and provide a good basis for comparison against standard bibliographies, reviewing sources, and other library collections.

The policy statement was written by the Collection Development Committee of the Irwin Library System in consultation with members of the Butler University faculty and with the advice and approval of the Academic Services Committee of the Faculty Assembly.

Butler University
Indianapolis, Indiana

I. Definition of Library Materials
   Library materials are print and non-print instructional and
   research materials (e.g. books, periodicals, pamphlets,
   manuscripts, microforms, aural recordings, etc.) organized
   and housed to support the aims and functions of the
   University.

II. Structure and Allocation of the Acquisitions Budget
    A. General Structure
       There are six line items established for library col-
       lection development. These are: Books, Serials, Scores
       and Recordings, Microforms, Non-Print Materials, and
       Binding and Repair. The budget for each item is estab-
       lished through recommendations for funding submitted by
       the Director of the Irwin Library System before the
       beginning of each fiscal year. These recommendations
       are arrived at on the basis of estimates of funds
       needed to continue acquiring library material at the
       current level, plus estimates of additional funds
       needed to improve the collections in specific areas and
       estimates of the anticipated rise in prices. Each of
       these funds may be administered in different ways
       depending upon the requirements for the various types
       of materials.

    B. Budget Line Items
       Serials
       Serials funds are used to acquire materials issued in
       successive parts, consecutively numbered, and intended
       to be continued indefinitely. Although treated as a
       unit, funds are accounted for by subject area so that
       expenditures remain balanced according to the level of
       collecting established for each subject.

       Scores and Recordings
       This line item is used to acquire musical scores and
       sound and video recordings for the library system. The
       funds are allocated to the Music and Fine Arts Library
       and Instructional Services based upon their estimates
       of collection need and available funds. Selection is
       coordinated by the heads of these library branches.
       Items recommended by faculty and staff are carefully
       considered and will be acquired as funds are available.

       Microforms
       This fund provides for the acquisition of all
       microforms for the library system including microform
       subscriptions to periodicals and microform sets. The
       budget is established based upon continuing current
       subscriptions plus funds needed for new titles or sets
       and the anticipated price increases. Selection is
       based upon faculty and library staff recommendations.
       Coordination is provided by the Collection Development
       Librarian.

Non-Print Materials

This line item provides for the purchase of various types of materials such as slides, filmstrips, kits, games, and other non-print format materials. These funds support the Curriculum Resources Center in Instructional Services as well as the non-print needs of the other libraries. Funds are allocated at the beginning of each year based upon estimated needs in each library and the availability of funds. Selection coordination is provided by the head of each department or branch receiving a portion of the line item.

Binding and Repair

This category supports the physical maintenance of the current print collections and rebinding or reinforcement binding of new materials that may not hold up under normal library use.

Books

Of the book budget, approximately fifty percent is for the general library collection (e.g. reference, standing orders, general books, indexes, replacements) and fifty percent is allocated to the academic subject areas.

The amount of the allocation will be determined by using five criteria in examining each subject area:
1. quality and number of books
2. number of full- and part-time faculty
3. number of new titles available
4. average price of books
5. number of student credit hours

Subject area funds are library funds allocated for departmental order recommendations. Recommendations against these funds may also be made by the library staff. Recommendations to order library materials may be reconsidered if the materials are inconsistent with the collection development policy or if funds are insufficient.

Funds remaining as of March 1 of each year will revert to the library's general fund.

Recommendations are received from faculty, staff, and students. All recommendations are considered in accordance with the level of collection development established for each subject area.

III. Acquisitions Policies

A. General

Underlying the acquisition decision making process for all types of materials are certain basic considerations:

29

Butler University
Indianapolis, Indiana

1. completeness of holdings as determined by standard
   bibliographies and other sources
2. considering each purchase in view of the library as a
   system
3. relative importance of all formats of materials for each
   department or branch library
4. faculty participation in selection
5. need for supplementing materials in subject areas of
   strong student interest or of a contemporary nature
6. study of use patterns (circulation statistics, etc.) to
   determine areas of great demand or areas in which the
   collection is weak
7. reviews in scholarly journals and other reputable
   publications

B. **Librarian and Faculty Selection Responsibilities**
   The responsibility for collection development rests with the
   library. The process of selecting material for the library's
   collections is a cooperative one involving faculty members
   and library staff. While there is no distinct division of
   labor, it is assumed that individual faculty members will
   work with the library liaison assigned to their discipline
   to select appropriate library materials. The librarians
   depend upon the faculty to provide subject and bibliographic
   knowledge needed to help evaluate the library collection and
   select additional titles for acquisition. Faculty members
   should consider not only the specialized needs of their research and courses taught, but also the general needs of the
   collection within the discipline as a whole, in related
   disciplines, and in interdisciplinary areas where they may
   have expertise.

   The library staff is prepared to assist the faculty in this
   process. This may be done by checking specific bibliographies for current holdings, establishing the availability
   of particular titles or sets for purchase or examination on
   location in a nearby library, or providing a current awareness service of titles recently published or reviewed. Any
   of these or other support services can be set up to assist in
   the process of collection development. All librarians are
   responsible for taking an active role in initiating purchases.

   A librarian acts as a liaison with each academic department
   or college. This librarian meets with the faculty of each
   area on a regular basis in order to exchange information
   about curriculum developments, library needs, and developments in the library such as new services, policies, and collection development activities. Each academic area's liaison
   librarian is the contact person for any questions or issues
   relating to the library and will make every effort to respond
   to requests and queries as quickly as possible. This
   librarian liaison will expedite the flow of information between faculty and library staff, thus enabling the library to
   provide better service to faculty. Of course, faculty mem-

bers are free to call upon any librarian for particular needs
best served by that staff member.

C. **Order Requests**
Both faculty members and library staff may submit requests
for purchase of all types of materials to the Acquisitions
Department on an official request form. These forms may be
obtained from any of the libraries. Periodical subscription
requests are submitted to the Serials Librarian; all others
are submitted to the Acquisitions Department. Those submitting requests are asked to supply as much information about
the title as possible. An authorized signature is required
on each form.

Requests are processed in order of receipt. Every effort is
made to place orders within two weeks. However, there may be
a delay with some orders since the sequence in which orders
are placed depends to some extent on the desirability of
batching requests so that a reasonably large order can be
placed with a vendor to obtain the best discount. Consideration will be given to expediting orders for urgently needed
materials.

Requests submitted simultaneously for large numbers of items
as part of a special collection building project will be
placed into the ordering schedule in a way which does not un-
reasonably delay the routine processing of departmental
requests.

Verification with respect to library holdings and accuracy of
bibliographic information must be made before any order can
be placed.

D. **Specific Types of Materials**
    Serials
Daily, weekly, bi-weekly, semi-monthly, monthly, quarterly,
tri-quarterly, bi-annual, and in some cases annual, publications are treated as serials. In placing subscriptions for
additional serials, a high degree of selectivity is mandated
by the multiplicity of new serial titles, the potential
obligation to maintain a serial in perpetuity, escalating
costs of serials, and cost of binding and maintenance.

Serials are selected and preserved to supplement the book
collection with current material in various subject fields
and to make them available for reference use on a long term
basis. Serials are not purchased on trial or solely for
recreational reading. Back files of serial titles are
selected based on the same criteria as current and new subscriptions and are purchased as teaching and research needs
require and funds allow.

Indiana newspapers are chosen to achieve selective coverage
of the state. National and international newspapers are
acquired on a highly selective basis to give balanced

31

geographical coverage. Priority is given to Indianapolis papers and consideration is given to titles of regional interest. Selected newspaper backfiles are retained exclusively in microfilm. Indexed newspapers are given priority due to their increased utility.

There are additional considerations in selecting serials and newspapers in microform: the need to fill gaps in serial holdings, to replace badly worn volumes, to acquire a second copy of a heavily used serial, and to conserve shelving space.

Maps

The map collection contains selected single sheet and portfolio, topographical and political maps available from federal depository and commercial sources, and other selected maps as needed to support the curriculum and degree programs of the University.

Scores

For purposes of this policy, a score is defined as any printed or mechanically produced notation of music. Scores are essential to the support of the curriculum and degree programs of the Jordan College of Fine Arts and are purchased in the following formats:

    scholarly editions of complete works of major composers
    scholarly collected editions usually of a specific genre or from a specific area or time period
    miniature (study) scores
    operas
    cantatas   [full score and piano-vocal score]
    oratorios
    Broadway shows
    other large vocal compositions
    solo instrument/voice with or without accompaniment
    duets with or without accompaniment
    small ensembles (3-10 parts) scores and parts

Multiple copies of choral music are not purchased with library funds, but those purchased by Jordan College of Fine Arts for the performing choirs are added to the circulating collection.

Orchestra or band performance scores and parts are not purchased with library funds nor added to the collection. A card catalog of the holdings of the symphony orchestra and the symphonic band is kept for the convenience of the patrons.

Manuscripts or photo reproductions of the manuscripts of Butler University alumni and faculty compositions are acquired whenever possible.

Microforms of scores are purchased only if the title is essential to the curriculum and is available only in microform.

Photocopies of scores are added to the collection only if they are produced in compliance with the current copyright law.

Butler University
Indianapolis, Indiana

Non-Print Media
Non-print media is an effective alternative to print media for
the dissemination of information in some subject areas. The
selection of audio-visuals is based on the same principles as the
selection of books. In addition, the following criteria are
considered:
appropriate academic level
technical quality of color, sound, continuity, etc. must be
   good
currency and timeliness of the materials
cost effectiveness
appropriateness of the audio-visual format in a subject area
strict compliance with copyright law

a. For purposes of this policy, a sound recording is defined
   as any device used for the storage of sound.

   The library acquires sound recordings of both music and
   the spoken word. Sound recordings of music are essential
   to the programs of the Jordan College of Fine Arts.

   Sound recordings of plays, poetry, dialects and sound
   effects support the curriculum and degree programs of the
   English, Speech, and Theatre departments. Recordings
   intended to teach a foreign language are not purchased
   with library funds. Tapes for that purpose are available in the language laboratory. Sound recordings of
   other spoken materials (speeches, lectures, etc.) are
   purchased if they represent the best source of information.

   Sound recordings are purchased in the format for which
   the best playback equipment is available.

b. Films and Video Cassettes
   Films and Video Cassettes are purchased that support the
   curriculum and degree programs of the University. They
   will not be added to the collection unless they were
   produced in compliance with the current copyright law.

c. Slides
   Good quality commercially available slides are purchased
   as necessary to support the curriculum and degree
   programs of the University.

Photographs, Posters, Prints
Photographs, posters, or prints may be acquired for specific
subject areas and special collections.

Vertical Files
Vertical files are maintained in various branches and departments
of the library system. These may contain clippings or
photocopies from newspapers, periodicals, pamphlets, ephemeral

Butler University
Indianapolis, Indiana

materials, and special project papers on subjects of current interest. The files are used to supplement the collections with
information not readily available in monographs or serials as
well as special materials unique to each library.

Paperbacks
Generally, hardbound editions are ordered for the library because
they are more durable than paperbound editions. However, if
there is a significant difference in price, a paperback edition
may be ordered. Paperback editions are bound or reinforced
either by the vendor, by a commercial binder, or by the library.
Other considerations besides price in choosing between hard cover
and paper editions include the following:
1. whether the paper edition is a tradebook or scholarly
    press title (scholarly press paper editions are generally
    more durable)
2. whether the title is of narrow interest and not likely
    to circulate frequently
3. whether the work is likely to be superseded or become
    outdated after a relatively short period of time

Special Papers
This is a catch-all category that includes a number of bibliographic formats sometimes considered as requiring special
policies. Included here are such things as dissertations,
theses, technical reports, proceedings, addresses, speeches, or
any other document not provided for by any other category listed
in this policy. The library does not exclude any format or document from consideration for acquisition.

Official Documents
a. Federal
    The Irwin Library System is a selective depository for U.S.
    government publications. The documents librarian, in con-
    sultation with appropriate faculty members, is responsible
    for the selection of depository series from those available.
    Selection is made on the basis of the University's instruc-
    tional and research needs, but also with some regard for the
    general information needs of the library's non-University
    patrons, whom Irwin Library serves as one of the depositories
    of Indiana's 10th Congressional District.

In supporting both reference and research with information published by the Federal Government, the library actively collects
statistical compendia, bibliographies, directories, annual
reports, compilations of laws, and Congressional publications.
Gaps in certain series are filled retrospectively by acquiring
out-of-print materials through offers lists received regularly
from other libraries. Documents contained in an unselected
series which are brought to the library's attention may be in-
dividually purchased through the library's GPO account or from
the issuing agency. To insure future receipt of similar publications, the depository series in question may be selected on a
trial basis.

Butler Univeristy
Indianapolis, Indiana

The library concentrates on maintaining a functional core literature of depository documents, while requests for more specialized
publications are referred to the Regional Depository (Indiana
State Library) or to interlibrary loan. Selection of new series
is carefully evaluated and currently active selections are periodically reviewed to determine the usefulness of a given series.
If even a few titles of a series meet selection criteria, the entire series is continued.

United States government publications are discarded in accordance
with Federal depository regulations.

b. State and Local
    The library is not a depository for state and local docu-
    ments, but will acquire them as curricular and research needs
    dictate. Priority is given to current editions of Indiana
    and Marion County documents, including statistics and legal
    codes.

c. Foreign and International
    The library is not a depository for foreign or international
    government publications. Publications of the United Nations,
    World Bank, International Monetary Fund, OECD, COMECON, and
    other international agencies are acquired if needed to sup-
    port the curricular and research needs of the University.
    Publications of foreign governments are acquired on the same
    basis.

Gift Policy and Procedures
The library will accept gifts of monographs, journals, music
scores, recordings, manuscripts, and other print and non-print
materials appropriate to the collections. Gifts may be received
at the Irwin Library or the branch libraries by any member of the
staff.

The library accepts gifts only on the condition that it may ap-
propriately exchange, donate, sell, or discard those items that
cannot be added to the collections. Before accepting gifts on
behalf of the library, staff members must ensure that donors understand and agree to this condition. If there is any question
about accepting a gift, the final determination rests with the
Director. Money received from the sale of materials is placed in
a fund for purchase of library materials.

The staff member accepting a gift must complete, in triplicate,
the Gift Material Acceptance Form, providing a full description
of the items. Official acknowledgment of the gift is made by the
University Relations Office. However, if the donor wants a
receipt, the second copy of the form may be given to him or her.

Guidelines for evaluation of gifts are the same as those for
selecting purchased materials.

The library cannot make appraisals. It abides by the Statement
of Appraisal of Gifts, approved by the Board of Directors of the

Butler University
Indianapolis, Indiana

Association of College and Research Libraries. (See APPENDIX D)

Gifts of money are used by the library to purchase library materials, equipment, or services. Donors of monetary gifts may designate the use of those funds for specific purposes through negotiation with the Director of the Irwin Library System.

Out-Of-Print and Retrospective Materials
Where requests or evaluation of the collection reveal a need for retrospective materials, the library attempts to purchase them through out-of-print dealers, who are usually given up to one year for their search. Microform or photocopies may be substituted for the original.

Rare and Archival Materials
Rare books, serials, scores, recordings, maps, prints, and manuscripts are acquired through purchase, gift, trade, or transfer in subject areas that augment existing special collections housed in the Hugh Thomas Miller Rare Book Room, the John S. Wright Great Books Room, the Judge Carl Rich Room, and other designated areas within the Irwin Library System. Emphasis is given to materials that enhance those special collections for which Butler University has acquired fame and to those portions of the collections that support teaching and research interests within the University community. Acquisition decisions are made on an item-by-item basis by the Rare Books and Special Collections Librarian in close collaboration with the Director of the Irwin Library System.

All materials that pertain to the history of Butler University are considered for acquisition by the University Archives: housed in and administered by the Irwin Library. Materials are acquired through transfer, gift, and occasional purchase. Acquisitions decisions are made by the Rare Books and Special Collections Librarian, in close collaboration with administrative and faculty offices and the Director of the Irwin Library System, in accordance with the Guidelines for Butler University Archives. (See APPENDIX G).

Textbooks
The library does not normally purchase textbooks, accompanying manuals, workbooks, and other auxiliary materials. They are considered to be secondary sources of information written and arranged specifically for the purpose of instruction and are generally state-of-the-art surveys which tend to become outdated rapidly. Exceptions are made for textbooks which are recognized as standard reference and review sources or represent the best source of information available on a subject.

Popular Materials
Popular paperbacks are purchased from gift funds designated for that purpose and are housed in the Caldwell Browsing area or other appropriate places.

Butler University
Indianapolis, Indiana

Research Materials
The library supports graduate level research in all subject areas
in which a graduate degree is offered. Bibliographic and
reference tools which assist in post-masters and faculty research
are also purchased depending on need and availability of funds.

E. **Levels of Collection Development by Subject Classification**
The Association of Research Libraries has developed a system
of "Collecting Level Codes" to be used for their National
Collections Inventory Project. The Irwin Library System has
adopted these codes to define the level of collecting for
which we should strive in order to support adequately the
academic programs offered by the University and to meet the
information and research needs of our students and faculty.
These codes are:
0 - Out of Scope. Not collected.
1 - Minimal Level. Very basic works only.
2 - Basic Information Level. Up-to-date general
materials that introduce and define a subject;
basic reference works.
3 - Instruction Support Level. Supports undergraduate
and most graduate instruction or sustained independent study.
4 - Research Level. Major published sources, including
journals, required for dissertations and independent
research.
5 - Comprehensive Level. All significant works of
recorded knowledge in all applicable languages; a
"special collection" aiming at exhaustiveness.

A basic outline of the Library of Congress Classification
System is used to describe the subject arrangement of knowledge available to the library. Each LC Classification area
is assigned an appropriate level of collecting. This level
of collecting is used as a guide to assist in the full
development of the collections. (See APPENDIX A)

IV. **The Reference Collections**
The reference collections are non-circulating collections
of materials designed to meet the basic research, verifica
tion, location, and information needs of the University
community in all subject fields. Reference materials of
all types and in all languages are selected in accordance
with the criteria established for the selection of library
materials. The works chosen for the reference collection
supply as much reliable information as possible with a
minimum of duplication. As a general rule, only the latest
edition of a reference work is shelved in the reference
section. Older editions are transferred to the general
circulating collection or weeded from the collection.

A. **Irwin Library**
The Irwin Library reference collection supports the

37

curriculum, degree programs and faculty research of the
University colleges not covered in the Music and Fine
Arts or Science Libraries.

1. Encyclopedias
   The collection contains appropriate general encyclopedias which are updated on a rotating schedule and
   and subject encyclopedias which are updated as new
   editions become available. New purchases follow the
   library acquisitions policy.

2. Dictionaries
   English language, foreign language and subject
   dictionaries are purchased in accordance with acquisition policies. They are updated if they become
   obsolete and a new edition is avilable.

3. Indexes
   Subscriptions to general and subject indexes, indexes to book reviews and to works in collections are
   acquired to provide access to periodicals, newspapers, and some books. Standard indexes are kept
   current and new indexes are acquired when they
   complement library holdings.

4. Bibliographies
   Standard bibliographies, general bibliographies, and
   specialized subject bibliograhpies which can be used
   for general reference purposes are acquired for the
   Reference Department and do not circulate. Other
   bibliographies, including most author bibliographies, are acquired for the general circulating
   collection.

5. Directories
   Current directories, both general and subject
   oriented, are provided as basic research tools.
   Appropriate new directories are added as they become
   available.

6. Annual Reports
   From standard lists of corporations, annual reports,
   10k's and supplementary reports are requested to
   support specific courses in the College of Business
   Administration and general business research.

7. Legal Collection
   In addition to basic legal reference sources, the
   legal collection contains Indiana and federal law
   sources which support the curriculum specifically
   for the paralegal programs, business law and tax
   accounting. New acquisitions follow general
   policies.

8. Online Database Searching
   The Reference Department offers computerized literature searching through selected vendors to Butler
   students, staff and faculty who may request a search
   when their research needs cannot be reasonably met
   by using manual sources. The library reserves the
   right to impose limits on the cost of the search and
   to refuse a request if it is inappropriate for the
   computer method of information retrieval.

Butler University
Indianapolis, Indiana

9. College Catalogs
   To aid students in their choice of graduate or summer
   courses, and to aid faculty and administrators to
   research other institutions, the Reference Department
   acquires graduate and undergraduate college catalogs as
   well as current college directories.

10. Career Collection
    This small but growing collection is comprised of books
    and pamphlets to help students choose careers and find
    employment. It is developed in cooperation with the
    Office of Career planning and Placement. Acquisitions
    policies are evolving as needs are evaluated.

11. Vertical File
    The vertical file in the Reference Department consists of
    mostly ephemeral pamphlets, news clippings, and miscel-
    laneous items which are judged to be of supplemental
    value to the general library holdings. Usually nothing
    over fifty pages long is included in the file. There is
    an emphasis on the current popular topics needed for
    Speech and English students and on information about
    Indiana and Indianapolis.

B. Music and Fine Arts Library

The Music and Fine Arts reference collection supports the curriculum and degree programs of the Jordan College of Fine Arts
(art history, arts administration, dance, applied music, music
education, radio/tv, and theater).

1. Encyclopedias
   The most recent subject encyclopedias appropriate for undergraduate and graduate use are acquired. One current
   general encyclopedia is provided for the convenience of
   the patrons.

2. Dictionaries
   The collection provides a University-level English
   language dictionary and dictionaries of the major foreign
   languages in addition to appropriate subject specific
   dictionaries (e.g. musical terms, musical themes).

3. Thematic Indexes
   The collection includes thematic indexes of all major
   composers that are available. When more than one thematic
   index of a composer's works is available, the library
   acquires the one used by the Library of Congress first.

4. Indexes
   In order to provide access to the periodical literature,
   the library acquires indexes which cover the subject areas
   of the Jordan College of Fine Arts curriculum. In
   addition, the library acquires indexes to works in collections and anthologies, reproductions of art works, bibliographies of composers, and record reviews.

5. Bibliographies
   Bibliographies of literature or individual instruments and
   voices, large and small instrumental ensembles, and vocal
   ensembles are purchased. Bibliographies of literature on
   arts administration, dance, drama, music theory, music

39

education, music and dance therapy, radio/television, and
other subjects important to the music and fine arts
collection are acquired when available. Discographies of
recordings of individual instruments, genres, and
ensembles are also acquired
6. Scores
Scholarly complete editions of the works of major composers and scholarly collected editions of specific genre,
historical era, or geographic area are also a part of the
reference collection.
7. Programs
A collection of bound programs of performances by faculty
and students of the Jordan College of Fine Arts is maintained.

C. Science Library
The Science Library reference collection supports the curriculum
and degree programs in the departments of Chemistry, Biological
Sciences, Physics, Mathematics, Computer Science, the College of
Pharmacy, and the Holcomb Research Institute.
1. Encyclopedias
The most recent appropriate subject encyclopedias are
acquired. One current general encyclopedia is acquired.
2. Dictionaries
The science collection provides a University-level
English language dictionary and dictionaries of some
foreign languages in addition to appropriate subject
specific dictionaries (e.g. medical, pharmaceutical).
3. Indexes and Abstracts
In order to provide access to the periodical literature,
the library acquires a variety of subject specific
indexes and abstracts.
4. Directories
The Science Library acquires current directories of
health organizations as available.
5. Online Database Searching
The Science Library offers database searching through
selected vendors.

V. Special Collections

A. Hugh Thomas Miller Rare Book Room
The collections housed in the Rare Book Room include
books, manuscripts, serials, scores, sound recordings,
prints, maps, microforms, and ephemera in all fields of
liberal arts and sciences, pharmacy, the fine and
performing arts, education, and physical education. In
addition to the general Rare Book Room collections in
these fields, there are several special collections.
1. The William F. Charters South Seas Collection
The collection includes more than 2,700 titles.
Materials range from early circumnavigators' and
explorers' accounts to later detailed studies in
anthropology, natural sciences, history, social sciences,
religion, literature, linguisitics, and fine arts. While

the collection is rich in bibliographic rarities, a
systematic effort is made to acquire current research
and reference materials.
2. The Harold E. Johnson Sibelius Collection
The collection includes scores, books, manuscripts,
articles, newspapers, microfilms, and ephemera. This is
the largest, most important Sibelius collection anywhere
outside Finland. Scores and secondary sources are
acquired to fill gaps and to maintain current research
value. Wherever possible, books are acquired in their
original language because English translations are often-
times condensed versions.
3. Lincolniana Collection
The collection includes 19th century and other rare
books, pamphlets, newspapers, manuscripts, and ephemera
relating to the life and times of Abraham Lincoln. It is
supported through the holdings in the Irwin Library's
general collections. Research and reference materials
are acquired to enhance the holdings.
4. The George Dellinger Collection of Early Educational
Materials Printed in the United States
The collection includes readers, primers, grammars,
mathematics, sciences, history, teaching methods,
etiquette, and related materials. Books and pamphlets
are acquired mostly through gifts.
5. American Popular Music Printed Before 1901
The collection includes more than 280 items of sheet
music. Additional music items are acquired through
gifts; some pertinent reference works are purchased.
6. The National Track and Field Hall of Fame Library
The collection consists of books, pamphlets, programs,
serials, and ephemera. It is maintained as a cooperative
effort between the National Track and Field Hall of Fame
and Butler University. At present, materials are
acquired through transfer from the Hall of Fame, and
gifts from members of The Athletics Congress and its
affiliate institutions.

The Hugh Thomas Miller Rare Book Room houses numerous smaller
special collections; Tibetan wood-block prints; engravings by
Piranesi, Wilson, and Cochin; wood-cut portraits of Butler
University faculty; papers and books from the library of Alice
Bidwell Wesenberg (20th century American poetry); a Madame de
Stael study collection; the country's largest Gaar Williams and
Kin Hubbard collection with many original drawings. Rare and
special materials are being added to all materials, including
pertinent reference works that do not duplicate reference collec-
tions in other parts of the Irwin Library System.

B. **University Archives**
The University Archives collect records, documents, and
publications of historical, legal, fiscal, and administrative
value to the University community. In selecting records, one
or both of the following criteria should be met:
1. The record should document the development and growth of

of the institution.
2. The record should reflect the development and activities
   of those offices and committees that cut across
   departmental divisions and that formulate or approve
   University-wide or college-wide policy as well as
   faculty, student, and administrative involvement in those
   activities.

In addition, the Archives may accept records in imminent danger
of loss or destruction for temporary storage, pending a decision
on ultimate storage or disposal.

The Archives collection includes, but is not limited to:
1. Annual catalogs, bulletins, baccalaureate and commencement
   programs, and other general publications;
2. Yearbooks, campus newspapers, and other serial publications
   produced by members of the University community;
3. Alumnal newsletters and publications;
4. Student, staff, and alumnal directories and handbooks;
5. Records of student, staff, and alumnal organizations and
   clubs;
6. University charters, by-laws, and amendments;
7. Financial records, president's annual reports, audit
   reports;
8. Board and committee minutes and reports;
9. Faculty and staff biographical files;
10. Faculty, staff, and alumnal publications;
11. Physical environment records such as photographs,
    blueprints, architectural plans;
12. Miscellaneous scrapbooks, clippings, photographs, and
    programs.

Currently, Jordan College of Fine Arts recital and concert
programs, photographs, and clippings are held in a special
archival section of the Music and Fine Arts Library.

Acquisitions for the University Archives shall adhere as
closely as possible to the policy guidelines of March, 1986
entitled "Guidelines for Butler University Archives,"
Section II B. (See APPENDIX G)

C. **John S. Wright Great Books Room**
   The Great Books Room houses a selection of finely bound or
   unusual sets of complete works and of famous works in the
   intellectual history of mankind. Walls and shelves are
   graced by busts of English and American authors and some rare
   paintings and engravings. Appropriate gifts are added to
   this collection.

D. **Judge Carl Rich Room**
   The Judge Carl Rich Room is designed to house the Judge Carl
   Rich Forensic Library as a distinctive scholarly resource for
   argumentation and forensics. A preliminary prospectus of
   recommended materials has been developed and is awaiting
   further study and review. The Delta Sigma Rho-Tau Kappa

V.

E. **Curriculum Resource Center**

It is the responsibility of the Curriculum Resource Center to serve the faculty, staff, and students of Butler University, particularly the faculty and students of the College of Education. The Center will attempt to provide materials needed to support the teacher education curriculum of the College of Education.

The Curriculum Resource Center will endeavor to collect a wide range of sample educational materials used in elementary, middle, and secondary schools in order to give education students the opportunity to study such materials by actually examining them, judging them, and then using those that they select. A good selection of textbooks and accompanying materials should be available, including as many examples as can be obtained of textbooks adopted by the Indiana Board of Education. Textbooks will not necessarily be excluded because they may be inferior to other textbooks, since it is part of the student's education to be exposed to all types of material and learn to choose the best of the items that fulfill their needs. Listings of textbooks adopted by Indiana and by various school corporations will be maintained.

Within the limitations of space and budget, the Center will attempt to provide student teachers with a wide variety of resource materials as well as instructional materials. Besides textbooks, teachers' guides, and workbooks, the Center will collect children's books, audiovisual items, and sources of general information that would often be used to supplement the curriculum.

A collection of children's books will be selected that are good examples of high quality children's literature, including the winners of the Newberry and Caldecott awards. Books that present accurate information about or portray varying ethnic groups or cultures will be collected to support multicultural awareness. Literature presenting handicapped children in a sensitive manner will also be represented to illustrate how books can be used to help children understand and accept handicaps. Some high-interest, low reading level materials will also be available.

Literature about the construction of curriculum and examples of curriculum guides and courses of study will be housed in the Curriculum Resource Center. Samples of curriculum guides prepared by Indiana schools will be available.

The periodicals in the Center will consist mainly of educational newsletters, periodicals that deal with current trends in education, and magazines that might be used by students in the classroom. Donations of more research oriented periodi-

Butler University
Indianapolis, Indiana

cals that are already available in Irwin Library are acceptable if
space permits.

The reference material in the center will consist mainly of encyclopedias and dictionaries that would be used in the school media center.
Indexes, directories, and bibliographies that might also be available
to teachers in the schools such as Children's Books in Print or the
Educators Progress Series will also be included.

A vertical file of ephemeral education-related material such as
pamphlets and newspaper clippings will be maintained in the Center.

Materials in the Curriculum Resource Center should pertain to
the practical applications of educational theory and knowledge to
problems of the school curriculum. No general education books will be
included unless they contain practical suggestions for applying the
information in practice. Duplication of items already available in
the Library System will be avoided unless library staff and College of
Education faculty agree that an exception is justified. Gifts of
library materials will be subject to the same selection criteria as
purchased items. The collection will be regularly weeded of outdated
materials and any others that are no longer useful.

Library materials for the Curriculum Resource Center will be
selected by the librarians in consultation with the faculty of the
College of Education, with the ultimate authority resting with the
Director of the Library. College of Education faculty recommendations, authorized bibliographies, personal examination of items, and
reviews from standard selection aids will be utilized in the selection
of the Center's collection.

Teaching materials and resources will be judged on the degree of ac-
complishment of purpose, the authority and competence of the author,
comprehensiveness in breadth and scope, objectivity, clarity and accuracy of presentation, potential usefulness, relation to the existing
collection and timeliness. Children's books will also be evaluated
for vitality, artistic expression, originality and imagination,
honesty and integrity, sustained interest, and consistency in charac-
terization.

Butler University
Indianapolis, Indiana

Alpha Archives are housed in this room.

VI. Maintenance of the Collections
A. Location
Library materials paid for with library funds must be
housed in one of the University libraries. Generally,
materials requested by a department will go to the
library housing that department's materials. However,
if the subject matter appears to be more appropriate to
another library's collection, it may be housed there.
The final decision rests with the Collection Development
Librarian or the Library Director.

B. Multiple Copies
Normally, only one copy of a title is purchased. Exceptions may be made to provide circulating copies of
selected reference books when there is high demand or
need for copies at more than one location or for reserve
purposes. Reserve copies will be ordered in accordance
with the objectives and criteria of the collection
development policy. Multiple copies will be acquired
when the class exceeds 40 students. Additional copies
are usually purchased in the most economical format.

C. Lost Items and Replacements
Resources that are missing, lost, or withdrawn because
of wear are not automatically replaced. Materials which
are known to be lost are replaced based on the following
criteria:
1. importance of the item to the collection
2. demand for the material
3. availability

A search for missing material is conducted for up to one year.
Materials not found during that time period are declared lost and
replacement is based on the above criteria. If there is high
demand for a missing item, a second copy will be ordered immediately while the search is continued.

D. Weeding
It is the responsibility of the library staff, in
cooperation with the faculty, to withdraw materials
which are inappropriate or damaged. The decision to
withdraw materials is based on the following criteria:
1. Circulation record of the item.
2. Completeness of holdings.
3. Availability of replacement for damaged item.
4. Importance of the item to the collection.

E. Conservation, Preservation, and Restoration
The library strives to maintain the physical integrity
of materials in the collection through conservation
measures such as temperature, humidity, and dust
control. Where preservation of content is more
important than the integrity of the physical format,

Butler University
Indianapolis, Indiana

materials are preserved by reinforcing existing
bindings, adding covers, or by microform.

VII. **Policy Evaluation**
The collection development policy will be evaluated and
changed as necessary by a committee appointed for that
purpose by the Library Director each year prior to the
allocation of funds to subject areas.

46

COLLECTION DEVELOPMENT POLICY

The planned development of a library's collection requires the application of a stated acquisitions policy. No policy can be definitive for all time, since a library is not a static institution. Ideas about its nature and content are constantly evolving. Therefore, a library collection development policy must be responsive to change.

The primary objective of Grasselli Library is to meet the informational needs of the faculty and the student body. The faculty have some research needs which must be met through use of other local libraries or interlibrary loan. Faculty members are strongly urged to distinguish between a research collection and one which is designed to meet the needs of our undergraduate and graduate educational programs.

The responsibility for the selection of the materials for the library's collection lies, in theory, with all members of the university faculty, librarians, staff, and students. Every effort will be made to accommodate requests which conform to stated policy. The library staff is charged with the responsibility of informing faculty and staff members of their rights and obligations in the area of materials selection. The various departments may opt to appoint one faculty or staff member to select in their respective areas, but it is strongly urged that individual faculty members protect their own interests and those of their students by staying abreast of the newly published materials in their particular areas of teaching and research. This helps keep the library attuned to curricular needs. The professional library staff will meet with new faculty and staff to acquaint them with general library services and also to promote input for collection development.

In accordance with the American Library Association Bill of Rights and the American Library Association Freedom to Read Statement, the library collection attempts to provide for the free exchange of ideas. The collection is available to all potential patrons of the library, and should offer the widest possible range of viewpoints; regardless of the popularity of these viewpoints, or of the sex, religion, political philosophy, or national origin of their authors.

In areas where there is an honest disagreement concerning the truth or wisdom of particular ideas, issues, or beliefs, and in the interest of reasonable economy, the library will attempt to see that the views of the best or major spokespersons are represented.

No censorship will be exercised on the basis of frankness of language, or the controversial manner an author may use in dealing with religious, political, sexual, social, economic, scientific, or moral issues.

In handling criticisms of material or attempts at censorship, the Library Director will reply verbally or in writing to the person or group, quoting or referring to the above policy. Persistent or repeated criticisms from persons or groups will be referred to the library's administration and the Library Committee.

Revised 12/1/87

John Carroll University
University Heights,   GRASSELLI LIBRARY
Ohio   ACQUISITIONS POLICY STATEMENT

The library will, as top priority, purchase materials in
direct support of the undergraduate and graduate academic
programs. In an effort to anticipate future needs and program
requirements and to purchase materials at publication rather than
retrospectively whenever possible, the library will use an
approval plan to augment regular orders. As previously stated,
faculty teaching and research needs will be met whenever
possible, given the long-term appropriateness to the collection,
relative price, and anticipated use of these materials. Book
reviews will be sought before ordering materials of questionable
value or high cost.
     Some types of library materials and services will not be
available at Grasselli Library. Patrons who require popular
fiction, some popular periodicals, and children's services will
find that the local public libraries effectively meet their
needs. Handicapped persons who need materials in a special
format not available in the collection will be well served
through interlibrary loan facilities.
     In the Cataloging area are a number of publishers'
catalogs and flyers, Books in Print, and other useful tools to
provide a means for the selection and evaluation of published
materials. The approval program is available to all selectors.
Those interested are welcome to make selections. Faculty and
staff are encouraged to send requests for materials which have
been reviewed in professional journals, etc., directly to the
Acquisitions Office. Students are welcome to submit requests
also.
     After a request has been made by faculty, staff or
students and submitted, an order will be placed for the material,
or the request will be placed in a desiderata file for such time
when it will be considered for purchase.
     Therefore, in an effort to develop and maintain a
collection of informational resources adequate in quality and
quantity for the varied learning and research needs of John
Carroll University, the following Library Collection Development
policy and guidelines have been adopted.

SPECIAL FORMAT STATEMENTS

     The collection of Grasselli Library will include all forms
of print and non-print materials.

1.   Newspapers - Newspapers will be added to the collection
if they significantly supplement the quality or quantity of
local, national, or international news available in those
standard newspapers already available. If major changes occur in
the quality or intent of those newspapers which have
traditionally been part of the collection, they may be re-
evaluated and/or discontinued.

2. Slides and Filmstrips - The library houses a collection of
several hundred slides and some filmstrips for use by students
and faculty.

48

Revised 12/1/87

3.   Sound Recordings, Tapes, Cassettes - The library will acquire
and maintain a reasonable collection of sound recordings. Tapes
and cassettes will generally be used for circulation needs,
thereby preserving the disc recordings.

4.   Works of Art, Photographs, etc. - The library will not
acquire, under present policy and guidelines, works of pictorial
or plastic art for viewing and/or circulation purposes.

5.   Maps and Atlases - A small number of maps will
periodically be acquired to supplement the collection of
governmentally produced maps available in the Reference Area.   A
reference and circulating collection of atlases is also
available.

6.   Pamphlets - Pamphlet requests will be dealt with according
to normal acquisitions procedures.

7.   Serials - In general, the same criteria will apply to the
selection of serial titles as for the book collection. However,
since every journal title represents a continuing expense, titles
will be added very selectively. Back files will be kept for
varying lengths of time depending on the subject. Microfilm will
be purchased rather than binding back issues for most titles.
The library staff or department faculty will periodically
evaluate the serials collection and discontinue titles no longer
needed, so that new titles may be added. Faculty and staff will
be notified of proposed cuts and their input will be sought.

8.   Government documents - Most of the documents the Library
receives are acquired through the federal depository system. The
library also receives a small number of United Nations, Canadian,
and OECD documents. These items will not be duplicated by
purchase for the general collection, except in a very few cases.
The Government Documents Librarian will determine what non-
depository documents may be necessary for that area, and will
submit those requests for purchase.

9.   Manuscripts and rare books - The existing collection
developed through donations of individual works or collections.
While we attempt to add selectively to the Chesterton Collection,
very few manuscripts or rare books will be purchased for the
library at this time.

10.   Microforms - The term microform encompasses the formats of
microfilm, microfiche, and microcard. These will be acquired as
needed. A primary reason is the saving of space. (see Serials)

11. Films, Videotapes & A-V Items - The contract with Kent State
AV Services does not prevent the library from selective purchase
of heavily used AV items. If a film or videotape is needed five
times or more in a year the library should purchase it. The
library will purchase other items selectively as funds permit.

Revised 12/1/87

John Carroll University
University Heights,   GRASSELLI LIBRARY
Ohio   ACQUISITIONS POLICY STATEMENT

POLICY GUIDELINES FOR MICROCOMPUTER SOFTWARE

Criteria for selection and retention of software shall
correspond closely to the criteria for selection and retention of
books and other library materials as outlined in the Book
Selection Policy of the library. Some specific distinctions are
covered in the following paragraphs.

1. **Demonstration disks:** At any time, the library may purchase
or otherwise procure demonstration disks of programs which may be
useful to the collection.

2. **Programs on approval:** At any time the library should order
programs for a limited time trial at the request of users in the
university community or on their own. These programs must be
returned promptly before the trial period expires.

3. **Public Domain Programs:** These should be procured from
whatever source and listed for use by the university community.

4. **Copyright Compliance:** Strict controls will be employed to
insure that no piracy of copyrighted programs occurs. A sign
placed on each microcomputer warning not to pirate programs is
the usual method to avoid problems

****

ADDITIONAL GUIDELINES

1.   **Gifts** - The selection of worthwhile items from books,
periodicals, etc., received as gifts will be governed by the same
criteria that govern the selection of purchased items. The
library reserves the right to dispose of duplicate and unwanted
material as it sees fit. The library is not responsible for a
monetary statement to the donor for tax purposes, but will
acknowledge receipt of the gift.

2.   **Textbooks** - Textbooks are not normally acquired unless
they cover an area of interest for which there is no general
material available. They will occasionally be purchased for the
reserve collection.

3.   **Reserve materials** - If special materials are needed for
reserve purposes, and are not available in the general
collection, the library will purchase up to two copies of a
title, provided that the title in question is within reasonable
price limits when compared to the publication's cost and long-
term value. "Reasonable price limits" will be determined by the
library.

4.   **Paperbacks** - The type of binding on a book will not be a
consideration in the decision to purchase except that the library
will exercise judgements of economy when the item is available in
both paper and cloth bindings. Relative price when compared to
the perceived long-term value and use will be considered.

Revised 12/1/87

5.   Foreign language materials - As a general rule, very little foreign language material will be acquired, except for literary classics in the major languages, French, Spanish and German materials to support course offerings, and foreign language dictionaries and encyclopedias for the reference collection.

6.   Duplication of materials - In general, one copy of any individual item in the circulating collection will be considered sufficient. In certain areas, such as literature, if duplicates are available through gift sources, they will be incorporated into the collection. Outside of a few basic tools, there will not be widespread duplication. Multiple copies in the circulating collection will be determined by the library staff in consultation with the requesting faculty member.

7.   Selection of vendors - The selection of jobbers, publishers, approval plans, vendors, etc., will be left to library personnel. Emphasis will be placed on speed, accuracy, special services, and discount.

8.   ACRL minimal standards - The library must meet standards set by the American College and Research Libraries for academic library collections to ensure accreditation for the university.

COLLECTION DEPTH

The library's collection may be separated into several distinct parts; the general circulating collection, the reference collection, Special Collections, and the serials and periodicals collection.
The basic collection will be made up of the following:
1.   Those items which constitute required, non-textbook reading for courses.

2.   Supplementary and ancillary reading for the courses.

3.   A basic reference collection.

4.   A good-sized collection of current periodicals and their back files. In determining the levels of collection development appropriate for Grasselli Library, the following categories have been established. They are as follows:

LEVEL ONE: MINIMAL/BASIC REFERENCE LEVEL -- Only fundamental reference works containing general information on a subject, e.g., dictionaries, encyclopedias, surveys, bibliographies.

LEVEL TWO: SELECTIVE LEVEL -- This level includes slightly more than the basic level. In addition to reference works, it would include a small collection of monographs and journals for general coverage of the subject fields.

51

John Carroll University
University Heights, Ohio GRASSELLI LIBRARY
                          ACQUISITIONS POLICY STATEMENT

LEVEL THREE: REPRESENTATIVE/UNDERGRADUATE TEACHING LEVEL -- A
balanced collection that covers all aspects of a subject field
without going into great depth. In an academic library, this
would be a collection which provides support for an undergraduate
degree program in the field.

LEVEL FOUR: COMPREHENSIVE/BEGINNING RESEARCH LEVEL -- A large,
well developed collection that includes specialized books and
some journals on an advanced level. In an academic library, this
is a collection which provides at least adequate support for a
Master's program in the field.

The library will attempt to meet the guidelines set forth for
levels one through four in all subject areas. The level of
collecting for each subject area will be defined in the current
Approval Plan Profile. The profile will be reviewed at any time,
and revised at least once every two years to insure currency.

Revised 12/1/87

Loyola University
Baltimore, Maryland
Loyola/Notre Dame Library
1986

COLLECTION DEVELOPMENT POLICY

Introduction

    The purpose of a collection development policy is to clearly
state the principles and guidelines along which the process of
selecting and acquiring materials will proceed. It is useful both
in providing consistency among those who have responsibility for
developing the collection, and in communicating the library's
policies to faculty, students and other members of the colleges'
communities. It is understood that as the programs and other
information needs of the colleges change, so the collection
development policy must be altered to meet these changing needs.
All members of the colleges' communities are encouraged to
contribute their ideas concerning the nature and content of the
collection development policy.

Mission of the Library

    The mission of the Loyola/Notre Dame Library is to provide
the information services and resources required to meet the needs
of the educational programs and concerns of the College of Notre
Dame and Loyola College, Evergreen campus. One way in which the
library achieves its mission is by selecting and acquiring the
print and non-print materials necessary to support successful
educational programs for both colleges. In developing the
collection the library's top priority will be the purchase of
material that directly supports the needs of the undergraduate
and graduate students of the colleges. The library also
recognizes its responsibility to respond to the needs of the
colleges' administrations and staffs, and to provide general
information and recreational reading for all its users. While it
is recognized that faculty have research needs, the library
cannot expect to meet most of these needs through the collection
development process. Other library services, such as
interlibrary loan and computer database searching, will be
utilized in assisting faculty with their research.

    In fulfilling the curricular needs of the colleges the
library normally buys material reflecting a wide variety of
viewpoints on religious, political, sexual, social, economic,
scientific, and moral issues. No censorship will be exercised on
the controversial nature or unpopularity of an author's point of
view or mode of expression.

Responsibility for Collection Development

    While the library has ultimate responsibility for collection
development, faculty, staff and students of the two colleges are
encouraged to contribute to the building of the library's

Loyola University
Baltimore, Maryland

collection. Each academic department is asked to appoint a
liaison to work with the library staff in developing the collection in. the department's subject area. Every effort will be made
to accommodate faculty requests that are within the scope of the
library's collection development policy.

The Assistant Director of the library supervises the
collection development process. Other librarians with responsibility for collection development are the Acquisitions Librarian
(monographs and serials), the Reference Librarian (the reference
collection), and the Audiovisual Librarian (audiovisual materials).

The Acquisitions Librarian stimulates faculty input to the
collection development process by circulating reviews on cards
from CHOICE (a periodical for librarians in which all reviews
are written by faculty subject specialists), the New Book List
from Harvard's Baker Business Library, and approval slips from
Midwest Library Service to the appropriate departments. In
making their own selections for purchase the librarians consider
reviews in library publications, standard bibliographies, user
requests, course syllabi and reserve book lists.

Allocation of Funds for Library Materials

The Assistant Director, in collaboration with the other
librarians responsible for collection development and the Faculty
Library Committee, is responsible for determining how funds will
be allocated within the materials budget. Funds are allocated for
reference and general materials, processing and binding of
materials, as well as for the various subject areas taught by the
colleges. Subject area allocations are determined with the
assistance of a formula that takes into account enrollments, cost
of materials, and usage of materials. Adjustments to the formula
figures may be made in light of special considerations that are
not adequately measured by the formula. Each subject area
allocation includes funds for monographs, serials, and
audiovisual material.

SPECIAL FORMAT STATEMENTS

Serials

Serials are publications that are issued periodically and
are expected to continue indefinitely. Usually they have volume
and/or issue numbers. Serials include journals, magazines,
newspapers, newsletters, abstracts, indexes and annuals.

Since serials represent a significant and continuing

54

expense, requests from faculty or students for new titles will be
scrutinized more carefully than is the case with requests for
monographs. Most serials that the library acquires should be
indexed or abstracted in sources that the library owns. When
local indexing or abstracting is not available a serial will be
acquired only when there are assurances from faculty that class
assignments will be made directly to the serial, or when the
serial is of current general interest. Special interest recreational serials will normally not be acquired.

Sunday newspapers which are representative of the various
regions of the United States will be acquired, but not preserved,
to supplement the daily coverage of the Baltimore newspapers, New
York Times, Washington Post and Christian Science Monitor.
Additionally, a limited number of English-language foreign
newspapers will be acquired. Other more specialized newspapers
(e.g. Wall Street Journal) will also be acquired as needed to
support the curriculum.

Audiovisual Materials

The library will purchase audiovisual materials needed to
support the curriculum in all formats for which it has equipment
or facilities. These formats include disc recordings, audiotapes,
videotapes, films, filmstrips and slides. The library will not
acquire works of pictorial or plastic art, photographs, or
non-book curriculum materials, such as tests, toys, games or
kits.

The library will normally not acquire audiovisual material
except at the request of a faculty member. Requests for more
expensive material will be scrutinized more closely than requests
for inexpensive material. Factors such as potential use, published reviews, the quality of the product, and overlap with
material already owned will be considered. The library will
normally not purchase audiovisual material for recreational use.

The library does not produce its own audiovisual material
and will not pay for the rental of material to be shown in the
library. The library may choose to purchase an item for which
demand is great even if the item is available from a free-loan
source.

Phonodiscs are to be preferred over audiotapes for the
acquisition of recorded music, since the library does not have
stereo audiotape equipment.

Videotapes are to be preferred over films when there is a
substantial difference in cost.

Loyola University
Baltimore, Maryland

Printed Music

The library will acquire musical scores as needed to support
the curriculum. Scores are cataloged and integrated with the
monograph collection.

Maps and Atlases

The library maintains a small collection of maps, but does
not actively acquire this format. A representative collection of
general and specialized atlases will be acquired and maintained
in the reference collection.

Pamphlets

The library maintains a vertical file containing appropriate
pamphlets received as gifts, but does not actively acquire this
format.

Computer Software

The library does not collect general purpose software (e.g.
database managers, spreadsheets), but will buy software with
particular applications to the curriculum, provided that the
software can be used on publicly available hardware in the
library, and that the library can produce a back-up copy.

Government Publications

The library is not a federal or state depository and does
not maintain a separate collection of government publications.
Government publications, whether monographs or serials, are
acquired in line with normal collection development criteria and
are integrated into the general collection

Manuscripts and Rare Books

The library does not purchase manuscripts or rare books.
These formats will be acquired only as gifts.

Microforms

Microforms are acquired when necessary to preserve materials, to acquire back volumes of serials that are not readily
available in hard copy, and to acquire current material that is
not readily available on paper.

Loyola University
Baltimore, Maryland

Paperbacks

    Paperback monographs for the regular collection will be
acquired when hardback editions are not available or when there
is a significant price difference between the hardback and
paperback editions. In making a choice between editions the
Acquisitions Librarian will consider the size of the price
difference, the funds available, and the long-term value and
expected use of the particular title.

    The library will also purchase a limited number of mass-
market paperbacks for recreational reading. These will not be
bound or cataloged, and will not become part of the regular
collection.

                        ADDITIONAL GUIDELINES

Reference Collection

    The reference collection is composed of information sources
that are most successfully utilized in the library and which the
Reference Department needs close at hand to assist in responding
to information requests. With few exceptions reference materials
are not meant to be read continuously from beginning to end, but
contain relatively short and discrete articles or bits of
information which users will consult one or a few at a time.
Reference materials include, but are not limited to, indexes,
encyclopedias, handbooks, directories, dictionaries and compilations of statistics.

    Reference material shall be as up-to-date as is necessary
for the provision of current and reliable information. Superceded
editions that are removed from the reference collection may be
added to the circulating collection if the information in them is
not obsolete or likely to be misleading to users. General
encyclopedias shall be replaced approximately every five years on
a rotating basis.

Textbooks

    The library will purchase texts that are requested by
faculty and may accept as gifts relevant texts that are not
superceded by a subsequent edition. No attempt will be made to
purchase every text that is being used for courses at the two
colleges.

Foreign Language Materials

    The library will normally purchase foreign language mater-
ial, whether in monograph, serial or audiovisual format, only to

support the foreign language teaching programs of the colleges.
Foreign language material most frequently purchased will be
general newspapers, current interest magazines, literature and
literary criticism, cultural or descriptive guidebooks to foreign
countries, and audiovisual material. In purchasing feature films
(whether in film or video format) the library will prefer
subtitled over dubbed versions.

Duplication of Material

The library will normally buy only one copy of any item.
Exceptions may be made when expected use will be heavy or when
material is needed for reserve. Faculty requests for more than
two copies of any item will be scrutinized very carefully and
will be honored only when materials needed for reserve are to be
used by a sufficiently large number of students (normally one
copy is sufficient for 10-12 students). Duplicate material
received as gifts will be added to the collection if warranted by
heavy usage of the copies already in the collection.

Out-of-Print Material

Back issues of serials no longer available from the publisher will often be purchased from other sources, but out-of-
print monographs will normally not be pursued through the OP book
market except at the request of a faculty member.

General Fund

A general fund is used for the purchase of monographs and
serials of a general nature which do not logically fit within any
subject area allocation, and for the purchase of appropriate
materials in subjects that are not taught at the colleges. The
general fund is also used to purchase paperbacks for recreational
reading which are shelved in the browsing collection. Purchases
from the general fund may be initiated by any member of the
colleges' communities.

Gifts

The Assistant Director is responsible for the acceptance and
disposition of gifts. The criteria for acceptance of gifts are
the same as those governing the selection of purchased material.
Duplicate and unwanted material will be disposed of as the
Assistant Director sees fit, unless prior arrangements to the
contrary have been made. The library will not be responsible for
the appraisal of gift materials, but may at its discretion
provide donors with estimates of market value when that is
readily ascertainable.

Loyola University
Baltimore, Maryland

Weeding

The Assistant Director is responsible for weeding the
monograph collection. No attempt will be made to weed unique
titles (except for superceded editions) on the basis of lack of
use, unless their condition is poor and their potential usefulness is judged to be negligible. This policy may be modified when
space becomes more limited. The weeding effort will be directed
at duplicates or variant editions that are not needed.

Serials will rarely be weeded unless space becomes a
problem. The Assistant Director and the Acquisitions Librarian
will collaborate in determining whether a serial shall be weeded.

The Audiovisual Librarian and the Reference Librarian are
responsible for weeding their respective collections. Decisions
to weed will be based on obsolescence of material, lack of use,
physical condition and space constraints.

Collection Depth

In determining the levels of collection development appropriate for the Loyola/Notre Dame Library the following categories
have been established:

Level 1: Minimal/Basic Reference Level
Includes only fundamental reference works and selected
monographs to provide basic coverage.

Level 2: Representative/Undergraduate Teaching Level
A balanced collection that provides broad coverage of a
subject area. Indicates a collection that helps to support
an undergraduate program of teaching at one or both of the
two colleges.

Level 3: Comprehensive/Beginning Research Level
A large well-developed collection that includes general
and fairly specialized monographs and serials in a subject
area. Indicates a collection that helps to support a
master's program at one or both of the two colleges.

In the Library of Congress classification breakdown that
follows the following code has been utilized:

   * Level 1
  ** Level 2
 *** Level 3

Loyola University
Baltimore, Maryland

A
General Works

```
 *   AC   Collections
 **  AE   Encyclopedias (General)
 *   AG   Dictionaries and Other General Reference Works
 *   AI   Indexes (Note: abstracts and indexes are not classified)
 *   AM   Museums
 *   AN   Newspapers
 *   AP   Periodicals
 *   AS   Academies and 'Learned Societies
 **  AY   Yearbooks. Almanacs. Directories
 *   AZ   History of Scholarship and Learning
```


B
Philosophy. Psychology. Religion

```
 **   B    Philosophy (General)
 **   BC   Logic
 **   BD   Speculative Philosophy
 ***  BF   Psychology
 **   BH   Aesthetics
 **   BJ   Ethics
 **   BL   Religions. Mythology. Rationalism
 **   BM   Judaism
 **   BP   Islam
 **   BQ   Buddhism
 ***  BR   Christianity (General)
 ***  BS   The Bible
 ***  BT   Doctrinal Theology
 **   BV   Practical Theology
 **   BX   Denominations and Sects.  Except:
 ***       801-4795 Roman Catholic Church
```


C
Auxiliary Sciences of History

```
 *   C    Auxiliary Sciences of History (General)
 **  CB   History of Civilization and Culture (General)
 **  CC   Archaeology
 *   CD   Diplomatics. Archives. Seals
 *   CE   Technical Chronology. Calendar
 *   CJ   Numismatics
 *   CN   Epigraphy. Inscriptions
 *   CR   Heraldry
 *   CS   Genealogy
 **  CT   Biography
```

Loyola University
Baltimore, Maryland

D
History and Topography (Except America)

```
**   D    History (General)
**   DA   Great Britain
**   DB   Austria. Czechoslovakia. Hungary
**   DC   France
**   DD   Germany
**   DE   The Mediterranean Region. Greco-Roman World
**   DF   Greece
**   DG   Italy
**   DH-DJ  Netherlands and Belgium
**   DK   Russia and Poland
 *   DL   Northern Europe. Scandinavia
**   DP   Spain and Portugal
 *   DQ   Switzerland
**   DR   Eastern Europe. Balkan Peninsula. Turkey
**   DS   Asia
**   DT   Africa
 *   DU   Oceania
 *   DX   Gypsies
```

E - F
America

```
**   E    America (General) and United States (General)
     F    United States (Local) and America (Except the United
          States)
**        1-975  United States (Local)
 *        1001-1140  Canada
**        1201-3799  Latin America
```

G
Geography. Anthropology. Recreation

```
**   G    Geography (General)
 *   GA   Mathematical Geography
 *   GB   Physical Geography
**   GC   Oceanography
**   GF   Human Ecology. Anthropogeography
**   GN   Anthropology
**   GR   Folklore
**   GT   Manners and Customs (General)
 *   GV   Recreation
```

H
Social Sciences

```
**   H    Social Sciences (General)
***  HA   Statistics
```

61

Loyola University
Baltimore, Maryland

*** HB Economics
*** HC Economic History and Conditions. National Production
    HD Land. Agriculture. Industry
***   1-91 Production. Industrial Management
 **   101-1395 Land
 **   1401-2210 Agricultural Economics
***   2321-9999 Industry
 ** HE Transportation and Communication
*** HF Commerce. International Business and Trade. Business
       Administration. Accounting. Advertising.
*** HG Finance
 ** HJ Public Finance
 ** HM Sociology
 ** HN Social History and Conditions
 ** HQ Social Groups. The Family. Marriage. Women. Except:
***   503-747 The Family
  * HS Societies
 ** HT Communities. Classes. Races
 ** HV Social Pathology. Social and Public Welfare.
       Criminology. Except:
***   2350-2990 Deafness
 ** HX Socialism. Communism. Anarchism

J
Political Science

 ** J Official Documents
 ** JA Collections and General Works
 ** JC Political Theory
 ** JF Constitutional History and Administration. General and
       Comparative
 ** JK United States
 ** JL British America. Latin America
 ** JN Europe
 ** JQ Asia. Africa. Australia. Oceania
 ** JS Local Government
 ** JV Colonies and Colonization. Emigration and Immigration
 ** JX International Law and Relations

K
Law

 ** K Law (General)
  * KD Law of the United Kingdom and Ireland
  * KE Law of Canada
 ** KF Law of the United States
  * KG-KH Law of Latin America
  * KK Law of Germany

62

L
Education

```
***  L    Education (General)
***  LA   History of Education
***  LB   Theory and Practice of Education
***  LC   Special Aspects of Education
 **  LD-LG  Individual Institutions
```

M
Music

```
 **  M    Music (General). Instrumental and Vocal Scores
 **  ML   History and Criticism. Biography
 **  MT   Music Instruction and Study
```

N
Fine Arts

```
 **  N    Visual Arts (General)
 **  NA   Architecture
 **  NB   Sculpture
 **  NC   Drawing. Design. Illustration
 **  ND   Painting
 **  NE   Print Media
 **  NK   Decorative and Applied Arts
 **  NX   Arts in General
```

P
Language and Literature

```
 **  P    Philology and Linguistics
 **  PA   Classical Languages and Literatures
  *  PB   Modern European Languages (General). Celtic Languages
     PC   Romance Languages
 **       1-400   General
  *       601-986  Rumanian and Romans
 **       1001-1977  Italian
 **       2001-3761  French
  *       3801-3976  Catalan
 **       4001-4977  Spanish
  *       5001-5498  Portuguese
  *  PD   Germanic Languages (Old German, Scandinavian)
 **  PE   English Language
     PF   Teutonic Languages
  *       1-1558  Dutch. Flemish. Friesian
```

**   3001-5999 German
    PG   Slavic, Baltic and Albanian Languages and Literatures
*   1-1998   General. Bulgarian. Serbo-Croatian. Slovenian
**   2001-2850   Russian
*   3801-9678   Ukranian. Czech. Slovak. Polish. Baltic.
          Albanian
*   PH   Finno-Ugrian and Basque Languages and Literatures
*   PJ   Oriental Languages and Literatures. General. Egyptian.
          Hamitic. Semitic
*   PK   Indo-Iranian, Armenian, Caucasian Languages and
          Literatures
    PL   Languages and Literatures of Eastern Asia, Africa,
          Oceania
*   1-489   Ural-Altaic Languages and Literatures
*   501-699   Japanese Language
**   701-898   Japanese Literature
*   901-998   Korean Language and Literature
*   1001-2245   Chinese Language
**   2250-3207   Chinese Literature
*   5001-8844   Oceanic and African Languages and Literatures

*   PM   American Indian Languages and Literature. Artificial
          Languages
**   PN   General and Universal Literary History. Collections.
          Theatre. Motion Pictures. Broadcasting. Journalism
    PQ   Romance Literature
**   1-3999   French
**   4001-5991   Italian
**   6001-8921   Spanish
*   9001-9991   Portuguese
**   PR   English Literature
**   PS   American Literature
    PT   Germanic Literature
**   1-4899   German
*   5001-5110   Dutch and Scandinavian
**   PZ   Juvenile Literature

Q
Science

**   Q   Science (General)
**   QA   Mathematics. Computer Science
**   QB   Astronomy
**   QC   Physics
**   QD   Chemistry
*   QE   Geology
**   QH   Natural History (General). Biology (General)
**   QK   Botany
**   QL   Zoology
**   QM   Human Anatomy
**   QP   Physiology. Except:
***   306   Voice and Speech

***		351-430	Neurophysiology and Neuropsychology
***		460-471	Hearing
**	QR	Microbiology	

R
Medicine

**	R	Medicine (General)
**	RA	Public Aspects of Medicine. Except:
***		971-972 Health Care Management and Finance
*	RB	Pathology
**	RC	Internal Medicine. Except:
***		423-429 Speech Disorders
***		435-580 Psychiatry
*	RD	Surgery. Except:
**		99-99.35 Surgical Nursing
***		523-525 Cleft Lip and Palate
*	RE	Ophthalmology
***	RF	Otorhinolaryngology
**	RG	Gynecology and Obstetrics
**	RJ	Pediatrics. Except:
***		101-140 Hygiene, Mental Health and Rehabilitation of Children
**		245-253 Pediatric Nutrition and Nursing
***		496.A5-6 Dyslexia. Aphasia
***		.B7 Brain Damage
***		.C4 Cerebral Palsy
***		.C67 Communication Disorders
***		.L35 Language Disorders
***		.S7 Speech Disorders
***		.S8 Stuttering
***		499-507 Mental Disorders. Child Psychiatry
*	RK	Dentistry
*	RL	Dermatology
**	RM	Therapeutics
*	RS	Pharmacy and Materia Medica
**	RT	Nursing
*	RV	Botanic, Thomsonian, and Eclectic Medicine
*	RX	Homeopathy
*	RZ	Other Systems of Medicine

S
Agriculture

*	S	Agriculture (General)
*	SB	Plant Culture
*	SD	Forestry
*	SF	Animal Culture
*	SH	Aquaculture. Fisheries. Angling
*	SK	Hunting

Loyola University
Baltimore, Maryland

T
Technology

```
     T   Technology (General)
 **      1-54  General. History
***      55-60  Industrial Engineering
  *      61-173  Technical Education
 **      173.2-174.5  Technological Change
***      175-178  Industrial Research
  *      201-379  Patents. Mechanical Drawing
 **      385  Computer Graphics
  *      391-995  Exhibitions. World's Fairs
     TA  Engineering
 **      1-492  General. Human and Systems Engineering. Materials
           Science
  *      501-1280  Surveying. Structural and Transportation
           Engineering
 **      1630-1750  Digital Signals. Lasers
  *  TC  Hydraulic Engineering
  *  TD  Environmental Technology. Except:
 **      170-196  Environmental Pollution
 **      201-500  Water Supply and Pollution
 **      879-893  Air and Noise Pollution
  *  TE  Highway Engineering
  *  TF  Railroad Engineering
  *  TG  Bridge Engineering
  *  TH  Building Construction
  *  TJ  Mechanical Engineering and Machinery
 **  TK  Electrical Engineering. Electronics. Nuclear Engineering
  *  TL  Motor Vehicles. Aeronautics. Astronautics
  *  TN  Mining Engineering
 **  TP  Chemical Technology
 **  TR  Photography
     TS  Manufactures
 **      1-148 General
***      149-199  Product and Operations Management. Packaging
  *      200-2301  Other Manufactures
 **  TT  Handicrafts. Arts and Crafts
  *  TX  Home Economics. Except:
 **      341-641  Nutrition. Foods and Food Supply
```


U
Military Science

```
 **  U   Military Science (General) and History
 **  UA  Armies. Military Policies and Defenses
  *  UB  Military Administration
  *  UC  Maintenance and Transportation
  *  UD  Infantry
  *  UE  Cavalry
```

Loyola University
Baltimore, Maryland

* UF   Artillery. Except:
**   767 Nuclear Weapons
* UG   Military Engineering
* UH   Other Services

V
Naval Science

* V   Naval Science (General)
* VA   Navies
* VB   Naval Administration
* VC   Naval Maintenance
* VD   Naval Seamen
* VE   Marines
* VF   Naval Ordnance
* VG   Minor Services of the Navies
* VK   Navigation. Merchant Marine
* VM   Naval Architecture. Shipbuilding

Z

* Bibliography and Library Science. Except:
** 40-43 Calligraphy
** 657-659 Freedom of the Press. Censorship
   5051-8999 Subject Bibliography-classified with their
   subject, not in Z

Philadelphia College of Pharmacy and Science
Philadelphia, Pennsylvania

Joseph W. England Library

Collection Development Policy

INTRODUCTION

The basic goal of the library is to support the objectives of the
College by providing resources and services to meet the information
requirements of faculty, students, staff, alumni and others in the health
sciences community. That the current needs of the students and faculty
are the most important consideration is reflected in the first specific objective of the library: "to develop and maintain a collection of books,
periodicals and non-print materials necessary to support the instructional
and research programs of the College," and was affirmed in November 1982,
through discussions with the Faculty Committee on Library and the Dean of
Faculty. Secondarily, the library seeks to develop a collection that will
facilitate another library objective: "to share resources and services with
other institutions to the benefit of the health science community."

The purpose of this collection development policy is to provide
guidelines for selection of materials that are consistent with this goal
and these two objectives. Specifically, the policy should:

(1) Ensure that the library develops a collection
balanced according to the current needs and use
patterns of the faculty and students.

(2) Provide a means for allocating funds fairly.

(3) Provide objective selection criteria for persons
who select materials.

(4) Provide a means for interpreting the collection
to potential users.

The policy covers monographs, journals and the individual collections of (1) Reference, (2) Reserve, (3) Audiovisual, (4) Special Collections and (5) Vertical file. It includes microforms and media, as well as
print materials.

The collection will vary in comprehensiveness according to the importance of the subject area to the College user community. Consideration
will be given to the fact that there are in the immediate geographic locale
six large medical libraries, two major universities with strong science
libraries, a major university library only a few blocks away with strong

Philadelphia College of Pharmacy and Science
Philadelphia, Pennsylvania

humanities, social science, business and general holdings, and an effective
interlibrary loan network linking most of the libraries. The PCP&S library
collection is not designed to support all research needs in any area except
pharmacy and pharmacology. It should provide at least basic support in
other disciplines with the expectation that graduate students and faculty
will use area research libraries for in-depth research. The composition by
major of the 1983 freshman class can serve as a first approximation to
subject balance.

Freshman Majors	Percent
Biochemistry	3
Biology	7
Chemistry	3
Medical Technology	3
Pharmacy	64
Physical Therapy	10
Toxicology	9

The biochemistry major was added in 1983 and indications are that
in the near term Biology, Chemistry and Medical Technology majors will remain proportionally about the same, that Pharmacy majors will decrease in
terms of percentages, that Physical Therapy will expand rapidly and that
Toxicology will expand gradually. It is critically important to recognize
that the Biology, Chemistry, Mathematics, Physics, Humanities and Social
Sciences faculties provide a large amount of instruction to the other majors.
Additional important factors are the graduate curricula in pharmacognosy,
medicinal chemistry and pharmaceutical sciences, the Doctor of Pharmacy program and the pharmacy residency program. Graduate students require stronger
support in terms of library materials than undergraduates.

The ultimate authority and responsibilty for allocation of the library materials budget rests with the Director of Library Services who also
does most of the routine selection for the general collection. The Head of
Public Services is responsible for selection of reference books and the composition of the reserve collection, the Head of Audiovisual Services for the
audiovisual collection, and the Rare Book Librarian for the Speical Collections and the Archives. Faculty members, students and staff are encouraged
to submit suggestions for book and journal purchases and faculty are asked
to review all candidate purchases which are not considered absolutely
essential by the library staff.

COLLECTING LEVELS

The following level definitions will be used in the individual
policies.

(1) Comprehensive level - the collection of all significant
works in all formats for a defined field.

(2) Research level - collecting materials adequate for dissertation

69

preparation and independent research, e.g., important scholarly
works, reference titles, books and many journals.

(3) Study level - provides current knowledge of a subject for limited purposes; adequate for undergraduate or graduate coursework or independent
study.

(4) Basic level - a highly selective collection which serves to introduce or define a subject, e.g., the latest or best monographs, a
few major journals and some reference books.

(5) Minimal level - relates to a subject area generally out of scope.
Only a few basic works are collected.

JOURNAL COLLECTION

General Purpose:

The primary purpose is to collect journals of lasting scholarly value
to support the College's teaching and research functions. Secondary goals
are to provide limited materials for leisure reading and cultural enrichment
and to serve as a resource library for current and historical research.

Collection: The journal collection consists of the following:

Second floor: Journals shelved alphabetically in the stacks
               Leisure reading magazines
               Latest issues on racks
               Microfilm collections

First floor: Abstracting and indexing publications
               Current awareness newsletters
               Microfilm collections in alcove

About 800 currently-received journals are collected in the following
subject areas:

Pharmacy and Pharmacology   Research Level

Several major abstracting and indexing publications.
Several important current awareness publications.
All English language journals judged by the faculty to be important.
Foreign language publications covered in Index Medicus or Inter-
national Pharmaceutical Abstracts, and newsletters of a few major
pharmaceutical associations (10 year retention).

Medicine   Study Level

At least one major abstracting and indexing publication. The major
clinical medical journals such as the New England Journal of Medicine.
At least one major journal in each of the medical specialty areas

70

that relate to pharmacy. At least one major history of
medicine journal.

Chemistry   Study Level

One major abstracting publication. Two major
current awareness publications. All American
Chemical Society journals that are related to
faculty interests. Other journals to the study level.

Biology   Study Level

One major abstracting journal. Two major current a-
wareness publications. Other journals to the study
level.

General Science   Basic Level

All major general science journals such as Nature
and Science. All major popular general science
journals such as Scientific American and Science 83.
One major indexing publication. Two broad current
awareness publications.

Other Subjects	Specific A&I Service	Collection Level
Toxicology		Study
Physical Therapy		Study
Biochemistry		Study
Medical Technology		Study
Business & Mangement		Basic
Social Sciences	X	Basic
Humanities	X	Basic
Math/Physics		Basic
Library		Minimal
Leisure	X	Minimal

Rare Journals

Rare journals are not collected actively. They may be
retained if transferred from the general collection to
special collections, or accepted as gifts.

Reference Journals (Abstracting and Indexing Services)

Major services are collected so that there is at least one
printed source for every subject area. The print collection
is supplemented with available access to several hundred online
databases.

71

Philadelphia College of Pharmacy and Science
Philadelphia, Pennsylvania

Special Types of Materials Collected

Educational journals in subject areas, e.g., the Journal of Chemical Education.
Three daily newspapers. Several publications useful for book selection. Specialized abstracting and indexing services only very selectively.

Types of Materials Excluded:

Newsletters, except for those of major pharmacy associations.
Pharmacy current awareness publications that overlap with ones already collected.
Journals of use to only one person unless they are acquired for selection purposes.
Scholarly journals not covered in an abstracting and indexing service.

Procedures:

New journal acquisition and journal cancellation decisions are made when possible, on the basis of the following criteria. The criteria are listed roughly in priority order.

Stated faculty need (or lack thereof)
Cost
Overall budget situation
Use or use potential
Abstracting and indexing coverage
Subject content
Collection balance
Citation record
Publisher's prestige
Type of publication
Availability in area libraries

The Director of Library Services is responsible for journal selection. When a journal title is being considered for addition or cancellation, all faculty who have an interest in the area, as indicated by the faculty interest file, are polled. Each polled faculty member is asked for suggestions on who else might be consulted until all possibilities are exhausted. As a safeguard, the Head of Public Services reviews all addition and cancellation decisions made by the Director before they are finalized.

Difficult decisions regarding expensive publications are discussed with the Faculty Committee on Library and the Dean of Faculty. The opinions of appropriate faculty and library staff are sought regarding all new subscriptions and cancellations. Candidate new journals come to the selector's attention through faculty recommendations, direct mailings from publishers, lists of journals added by other libraries, and the journal reviews published every Fall in Nature.

Philadelphia College of Pharmacy and Science
Philadelphia,   JOSEPH W. ENGLAND LIBRARY
Pennsylvania

JOURNAL OR SERIAL REVIEW INFORMATION

____ REVIEW OF PUBLICATION CURRENTLY RECEIVED

____ REVIEW OF PUBLICATION FOR POTENTIAL PURCHASE

DATE OF REVIEW:_____

TITLE:_____.

INDEXING: ___ IM   ___ SCI   ___ BA   ___ CA   ___ IPA

CITATION FREQUENCY: ___ SCI IN ____ (YEAR)
                       ___ SSCI IN ____ (YEAR)

COST:_____

RECEIPT BY LOCAL LIBRARIES: ___ CP   ___ JEFF   ___ UP MED

___ UP   ___ DREXEL   ___ FI   ___ ____   ___ ____
_____
STAFF COMMENTS (INCLUDE DATE)

_____
FACULTY COMMENTS (INCLUDE DATE)

_____

DECISION:_____

73

Philadelphia College of Pharmacy and Science
Philadelphia, Pennsylvania

Weeding:

Detailed weeding procedures are contained in another document and so
will only be discussed briefly here. Basically, weeding criteria are similar
to selection criteria with the following additional factors considered:

Age
Space
Value to history of pharmacy
Completeness of holdings

Certain publications have limited long-range usefulness and so are not
normally retained indefinitely. Adherence to these retention policies is a
method of automatic weeding.

Publication Type	Retention Policy
Scholarly journals	indefinite
Abstracting & Indexing Publications	never weeded
Leisure materials	1-2 years
Non-pharmacy news publications	5 years
Non-pharmacy current awareness publications	6 months to 1 year
Newspapers	2 weeks
Pharmacy association newsletters	10 years
Library journals	5 years

As space becomes more limited it may become necessary to weed back
runs of scholarly journals as well. Weeding decisions will be made on the
basis of value of the individual journal rather than an exact cutoff by
date. The journal collection is weeded systematically every five years.

Funding:

Most of the journal collection is funded from the general operating
budget. About 50 (mostly foreign) journals are received in exchange for
the College publication, the American Journal of Pharmacy.

Very few other journals are received on a regular basis as gifts,
and journal gifts are not usually encouraged because of the problem of
unreliable receipt. The library staff donates a few library and information
related journals and casual gifts are kept for a brief time period.

74

October 1983

Philadelphia College of Pharmacy and Science
Philadelphia, Pennsylvania

MONOGRAPH COLLECTION

General Purpose:

The primary purpose is to collect monographs to support and supplement
the instructional and research programs of the college, thus serving the undergraduate and graduate students and the faculty. Service to the professional
health science community requires that a historical collection of key reference
books in pharmacy be maintained as part of the general collection.

Collection:

Monographs are collected in depth in proportion to areas of instruction
at the undergraduate and graduate levels. Monographic support for research is
in the areas of pharmacy and pharmacology. Key reference books are retired to
the general collection to provide historical data pertaining to drugs.

Types of monographs collected
include:

Textbooks
Continuations
Government Documents
Scholarly Works
Popular Works

Types of monographs excluded are:

Technical Reports
Dissertations and Theses (most)
Manufacturers Catalogs
Annual Reports

Subject areas in which monographs are collected are outlined below with
indication of the audience, collection level and the NLM/LC classification used.
Within the scope of audience, the difference between Undergraduate Major and
Undergraduate is whether a degree is conferred in that area. The collection
levels assigned reflect the reality of budgetary constraints.

75

Philadelphia College of Pharmacy and Science
Philadelphia, Pennsylvania

The three major lists are Books for College Libraries, A Basic
Booklist for Pharmaceutical Education, and the "Brandon" list which is
published periodically in the Bulletin of the Medical Library Association.
Also considered are previous editions of, and supplements to, monographs already in the collection which are evaluated for usage before purchase of
related publications. Multiple copies are purchased only after substantial
need is established.

Information about books for potential purchase is sent to faculty
members in their interest and instructional fields. A Faculty Interest
File is maintained to assist in this task. The responsibility for final
selection rests with the library director who considers the following factors in addition to the subject: price, previous acquisitions in each
subject area, the requestor, the publisher and book reviews. A hold file
is maintained for titles considered but not acquired.

Weeding:

The weeding of the monographic collection is accomplished through
several processes. Continuous weeding is maintained in all subject areas.
As new editions are received, previous editions become candidates for weeding. As part of the process of reclassification of the collection, duplicate and out-of-date copies of books are weeded and retention policies are
established as necessary. A major weeding project may be undertaken every
five years if necessary.

Initial characteristics that identify a candidate for weeding are:
1) date of receipt is six or more years ago; 2) has not circulated in more
than five years; 3) not listed in Books for College Libraries and other
standard core lists.

Candidates for weeding are then reviewed by the Director of Library
Services and the Head of Technical Services and the following factors are
considered: 1) subject area; 2) earlier or superceded editions of textbooks;
number of copies and total circulation among them; 4) prominence of the author;
5) physical condition; 6) previously shelved in the Reference or Reserve
collection; 7) relationship to PCPS; 8) availability of "better" books on
the subject.

These books may then be reviewed by other professional staff and/or
faculty. The Faculty Interest File is used to match subject area with faculty
and at least one faculty person reviews each group of books, making the final
decision.

Weeded books are officially withdrawn from the collection. Disposal
methods include: transfer to classroom collections at the request of faculty,
transfer to the Rare Book Collection, sale, a give-away truck in the public
services area, and exchange with other libraries.

Philadelphia College of Pharmacy and Science
Philadelphia, Pennsylvania

Subject	Audience	Collection Level	Classification Areas
Pharmacy	Undergraduate Major Graduate Professional	Research	QV
Biology	Undergraduate Major Graduate	Study	QH-QS
Chemistry	Undergraduate Major Graduate	Study	QD
Medicine	Undergraduate Major Graduate	Study	QW-QZ, W-WZ
Biochemistry	Undergraduate Major (Fall 1983)	Study	QU
Medical Technology	Undergraduate Major	Study	TN-TS, W-WZ
Physical Therapy	Undergraduate Major (begun Sept. 1982)	Study	WB300-964
General Science	Undergraduate	Basic	Q, QE, QT, S-TL, TT-V
Business & Management	Undergraduate	Basic	HA-HJ
Math-Physics	Undergraduate	Basic	QA-QC
Humanities	Undergraduate	Basic	A-BX, HM-PZ
Social Science	Undergraduate	Basic	C-L
Leisure	Undergraduate	Minimal	
Library Science	Professional	Minimal	Z

See Table 1 for the distribution of the collection in the summer of 1982.

Procedure:

Monographs for prospective purchase are primarily chosen from reviewing the following sources: National Library of Medicine Current Catalog Proof Sheets, Technical Book Review Index, professional library journals, book reviews in core medical and scientific journals, other pharmaceutical and medical school acquisitions lists and publisher-supplied announcements. In addition, recommendations are considered when submitted from faculty, staff and students. Periodically standard published core lists are consulted to ensure adequate coverage in all subject areas.

Philadelphia College of Pharmacy and Science
Philadelphia, Pennsylvania

Funding:

General library funds are used to purchase most monographs for
the collection. Funds are solicited from new course programs for the
purchase of monographs in those subject areas. There are no designated
amounts nor time periods for such arrangements. Final responsibility
for selection of books with these funds rests with the Chairman of
the academic department.

Gift books are accepted at the discretion of the director of the
library. A detailed gift policy describes this process in more depth.
Books are received gratis from the book review departments of the
American Journal of Pharmacy (PCP&S) and the Annals of Internal Medicine
(American College of Physicians).

78

General Purpose:

The Reference Collection supports the administrative, academic and research programs of the Philadelphia College of Pharmacy and Science by providing library resources related to its diversified information needs.
Reference books are usually consulted for brief, factual data rather than in-depth information. The specific aims of this collection are:

A. To provide a permanent collection of current reference materials in the pharmaceutical, medical and basic sciences.

B. To provide a core collection of non-science and general reference sources.

C. To facilitate the use of heavily accessed tools by placing them in a central location where library staff assistance is available.

D. To provide sources that enable us to meet the information needs of our in-person and telephone reference services.

Collection:

The Reference Section of approximately 1400 volumes is a noncirculating collection with only a few titles duplicated in other collections. Although most items remain on reference continuously, books are returned to the main collection when no longer needed or as a new edition is received.

Types of Materials Collected:

The Reference Collection is comprised of 10 numbered sections and one larger unnumbered general reference section. The sections and types of materials collected within each are as follows:

1. Serials Information
   directories of periodicals
   union lists
   periodical abbreviation lists

2. Book Information/Information Science
   style manuals
   library directories
   guides to the literature
   selected bibliographies

3. Dictionaries
   English language dictionaries
   English-foreign language dictionaries
   specialized and technical dictionaries
   thesauri
   usage books
   medical and scientific dictionaries
   abbreviation and acronym books

4. Encyclopedias
   general knowledge encyclopedias
   single volume encyclopedic works

5. Directories
   Pharmaceutical and chemical manufacturers' directories
   general corporate directories
   medical and health related directories
   grant and foundation directories

Philadelphia College of Pharmacy and Science
Philadelphia, Pennsylvania

5. Directories (continued)
   Who's Who
   Governmental directories
   Educational sources

6. Pharmacy Information
   Pediatric drug handbooks
   Consumer guides to drugs
   Basic sources on teratogenicity
                     adverse effects
                     drug interactions
   Cancer therapy sources
   Other general drug information sources

7. Current Awareness
   Legal sources
   Unlisted Drugs
   Current newsletters

8. Ready Reference
   U.S. drug identification tools
   Foreign drug indentification tools
   Tablet/capsule identification tools
   Basic pharmacy reference tools

9. DeHaen
   DeHaen printed tools

10. Pharmacopoeias/Codexes
    Foreign pharamcopoeias and codexes

Unnumbered Reference Section
   Biographical sources   Carcinogen listings
   Author and literature series   Patent indexes
   Quotation books   CRC handbooks
   Poisoning/toxicology books   Specialized chemical series
   Food/nutrition sources   Education guides
   Homeopathic books   Almanacs
   Herbals   Etiquette books
   Veterianry sources   Basic science reference tools
   Pesticide books   College catalogs
   History of medicine

Additional collections housed in the reference area include:

   Atlas table
   U.S. and world atlases

   Index table
   Index Medicus
   Science Citation Abstracts
   Books in Print
   Jim List and other journal location tools

   Reference Desk
   Telephone books
   POISINDEX
   DRUGDEX

Reference Desk (continued)
Red Book/Blue Book
Chemical/drug catalogs
older editions of pharmaceutical sources

Abstracts and Indexes
current year and most recently bound volume

Types of Materials Excluded:

Nonprint format material

Procedure:
The reference staff is responsible for the selection and updating of
reference materials under the direction of the Head of Public Services.
New reference books are identified by reviewing:

> faculty and staff recommendations
> booklists from other institutions
> newly received/ordered books
> professional journals
> publishers' brochures
> Unlisted Drugs

College catalogs for U.S. medical, osteopathic and pharmacy schools as
well as selected local colleges are requested annually.

Weeding:
The collection is weeded on an ongoing basis as new editions are received
and older ones are removed from reference. A complete inventory of the
reference collection should be done each year by the reference staff.
The Head of Public Services then reviews the collection and weeds inappropriate or outdated titles. Faculty and library staff input is requeste
when necessary. Superceded editions of titles are not retained in the
Reference Collection. Such titles are evaluated for their continued
usefulness in the main collection, particularly for historical purposes.
Generally older editions of pharmaceutical reference books are retained
in the general collection while only the previous edition of non-science
and general reference sources are kept. Certain titles lend themselves
to individual decisions.

Funding:
General library funds are used to purchase materials for Reference. However
some expensive specialized tools are supported by a separate drug informatio
budgetary item. Reference does accept some gift items from the faculty.

Philadelphia College of Pharmacy and Science
Philadelphia, Pennsylvania

RESERVE COLLECTION

General Purpose:
The Reserve Collection supports the instructional program of the Philadelphia College of Pharmacy and Science by providing library resources
which are directly related to curricular offerings. The specific aims
of this collection are:
A. To provide reserve materials as required or recommended
by the faculty for student use.
B. To provide a permanent collection of core materials in the
pharmaceutical, medical and basic sciences.
C. To provide controlled use of materials whose format, value
or high demand may make them candidates for theft.

Collection:
The Reserve Section is primarily a collection of books which are borrowed
from the general collection and are returned when no longer needed or
a new edition is received. However, most items remain on reserve continuously. Reserve materials may be used only in the library. A few selected
sources of which we have duplicate copies may circulate overnight.

Types of Materials Collected:
In addition to course related books and periodical articles placed on
reserve by faculty, the collection houses the following:

course textbooks	resume guides
State Boards of Pharmacy materials	pharmacy residency materials
legal sources	historical sources
Ciba collection	core medical texts
pathfinders	botany/pharmacognosy books
core pharmacy texts	examination review books
	basic nursing texts

Types of Materials Excluded:

PCPS examinations
nonprint format material

Procedure:
Faculty, College personnel and professional library staff may request
that materials be placed in this collection, but ultimate responsibility
for selection lies with the Head of Public Services. New reserve books
are also identified by reviewing:

PCPS bookstore list
new course information
booklists from other institutions
newly ordered/received books
professional journals
publishers' brochures

Philadelphia College of Pharmacy and Science
Philadelphia, Pennsylvania

Updates to the State Boards of Pharmacy materials are requested
biannually. Some general policies which govern the collection
include:
- A. Faculty are responsible for providing appropriate
  number of copies of photocopied materials in
  accordance with the copyright law.
- B. Cooperation with the Technical Services Department
  to obtain reserve materials.
- C. Adding personal copies including photocopies which
  are in compliance with the copyright law when the
  library does not own a copy or cannot supply
  sufficient copies.

Weeding:

The collection is weeded on an ongoing basis as new editions are
received and older ones are removed from reserve. At the end of
each semester, photocopied reserve materials are returned to the
faculty member. A complete inventory of the reserve collection
is done each semester by the circulation assistant. The Head
of Public Services then reviews the collection and weeds inappropriate or outdated titles. Faculty input is requested
when necessary.

Funding:

General library funds are used to purchase materials for Reserve.
Reserve does accept some gifts and loan items from the faculty.

Philadelphia College of Pharmacy and Science
VERTICAL FILE
General Purpose:
   The Vertical File serves as a repository of ephemeral pharmaceutical
   and medical information that supports the information needs of the PCPS
   community.

Collection:
   The Vertical File consists primarily of brochures, pamphlets and articles
   on various topics. Monographs of potential interest but not enough
   permanent value to warrant cataloging are sometimes included in this file.
   A subset of this public file is the Reference Vertical File which is
   used primarily by the reference staff. This file contains information
   on frequently asked questions and timely topics.

Types of Materials Collected:
   Pharmaceutical Company annual reports and other selected information
   government publications
   statistical sources
   PCPS information
   historical information related to pharmacy, drugs and medicine
   pharmaceutical associations' publications
   brochures of health related clearinghouses, agencies and institutions.
   NLM Literature Searches
   National Center for Health Statistics publications including <u>Vital and
      Health Statistics Series</u>
   Clinical brochures on antineoplastic agents
   Pharmaceutical, medical and chemical symbols
   academic association information
   general interest brochures
   Philadelphia/regional information
   library and information science related brochures including those of
      national libraries
   copyright information

Types of Materials Excluded:
   Nonprint format material
   Monographs of permanent value unless duplicated elsewhere in the collection

Procedure:
   The reference staff is responsible for the selection of vertical file
   materials under the direction of the Head of Public Services. Vertical
   file material is identified by reviewing:

             faculty and staff recommendations
             newly received materials/books
             professional journals
             unsolicited materials

   The annual reports of pharmaceutical companies are requested annually.

Weeding:
   The Vertical File is weeded every other year under the direction of the
   Head of Public Services. The Reference Vertical File should be weeded
   each year.
Funding:
   Most materials in the Vertical File are received gratis from faculty or
   various agencies or institutions. Based on scope, decisions are made by
   the reference staff to retain or discard unsolicited material. Occasionall
   library funds may be used to purchase materials.

Philadelphia College of Pharmacy and Science
Philadelphia, Pennsylvania

AUDIOVISUAL COLLECTION

General Purpose:

The audiovisual collection supports the instructional programs at the
Philadelphia College of Pharmacy and Science by providing media for individual, small group and classroom use.

Collection:

The collection consists of commercially prepared materials in a variety of
formats as well as audio and video recordings produced on campus.

Types of Materials Collected:

3/4" and VHS video cassette tapes   filmstrip/tape programs
audiocassette tapes   filmstrips
slide/tape programs   overhead transparencies
35mm slides   33 1/3 rpm records
16mm films

When an item is available in multiple formats, videotape or slide/tape
programs are preferred.

In addition to audiovisuals, the collection houses some print materials
including media catalogs and basic texts on audiovisual production and
media management.

Types of Materials Excluded:

½" Betamax

Procedures:

Audiovisual materials which have been recommended by faculty or staff members
are previewed by at least one faculty member. Programs receiving positive
evaluations from faculty previewers are considered for purchase based
upon relevance to the curriculum, anticipated number of showings per year,
technical quality and cost. The Head of Audiovisual Services is ultimately
responsible for selection decisions.

Weeding:

Audio and video recordings produced on campus are weeded at the end of each
semester. The rest of the collection is reviewed by the Head of Audiovisual
Services as necessary to remove items which no longer meet the needs of the
instructional programs. Appropriate faculty members are consulted.

Funding:

The audiovisual budget is used to purchase materials for the collection.
The AV Center accepts some gift items.

Philadelphia College of Pharmacy and Science
Philadelphia, Pennsylvania

SPECIAL COLLECTIONS

General Purpose:

     To support historical research and provide library resources on
the history of the college and pharmacy.

Collection:

     The Special Collections consist of approximately 2,240 historical
and rare books which were donated to the library by alumni, faculty and
friends of the college. The majority came from the estate of a former dean
of the college, Dr. Charles H. La Wall. Others are from personal libraries
of the famous nineteenth century physician, Dr. John Redman Coxe and a
former Johnson & Johnson executive, Dr. Fred B. Kilmer. Pharmaceutical
ephemera are being donated by Dr. William Helfand, senior vice president,
Merck, Sharpe & Dohme, International.

Types of Material Collected:

     1. Books on medical botany, medicinal chemistry, pharmacology,
        pharmacognosy and pharmacy.

     2. Books on the history of pharmacy.

     3. Pharmacy journals of only historical value

     4. Complete sets of the National Formulary, United States Dispensatory,
        and the United States Pharmacopoeia. European dispensatories and
        pharmacopoeias are also being collected.

     5. Pharmaceutical ephemera such as price lists, advertising literature,
        almanacs, stock certificates, etc.

     6. Biographies of leaders in pharmacy.

     7. Pharmaceutical text books: for example a complete set of
        Remington's Pharmaceutical Sciences.

     8. Histories of colleges of pharmacy.

     9. Substantial and noteworthy presentation copies.

    10. Classics in the fields of the history of medicine and basic
        chemistry.

    11. Catalogs of historical collections.

Multiple copies of only high priority items are kept.

Philadelphia College of Pharmacy and Science
Philadelphia, Pennsylvania

Types of Material Excluded:

Because of the closeness of the History of Medicine Collection
at the College of Physicians of Philadelphia, the Institute of Chemistry
at the University of Pennsylvania and the Academy of Natural Sciences,
the decision has been made not to actively collect books in the following
subjects: medicine, non-medicinal chemistry, and the natural sciences
other than botanicals.

Procedures:

The Rare Book Librarian is responsible for collection development
for Special Collections. Rare Book Dealer Catalogs are scanned for
suggestions subject to the approval of the Director of Library Services.

Weeding:

As necessary.

Funding:

Additions to this collection are through gifts, contributions from
the Friends' of the Library and retirement from the General Collection.

Wilkes College

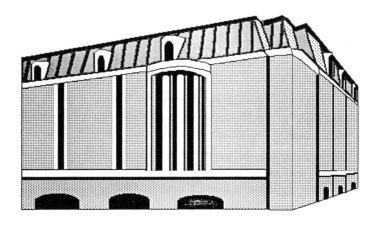

E.S. Farley Library

COLLECTION DEVELOPMENT POLICY

Wilkes College,
Wilkes Barre, Pennsylvania

Introduction

The Farley Library exists to support the total program of Wilkes College. Its collection should, therefore, reflect the curricular and research needs of the students, faculty and staff. Because the library cannot completely satisfy all informational needs of all users, a consistent and conscious effort must be made to provide the resources required by the majority of library patrons. This policy is intended to guide the building and enrichment of the collection in accordance with the mission of Wilkes College. The library staff, in consultation with the faculty, will continue to develop and modify this policy to meet the changing demands of Wilkes and the region.

Each academic department is allocated a portion of the funds provided to the library by the college administration for collection development. Though library staff members are responsible for the overall management and development of the library collections, faculty in all disciplines of the college are expected to take an active role in selecting library print and media materials. Faculty members may submit requests for materials in their fields or in other areas of interest according to the guidelines contained in the "Library Policies Manual." All materials purchased in this manner are charged against the appropriate academic department's portion of the library budget. Materials purchased with library funds become college and library property. Professional librarians act as contact persons or liaisons for each of the academic departments and can assist faculty with library resource selection and use.

Students, college staff, and administrators are also encouraged to make recommendations for book and media purchases to the library staff. Requests for purchase of library materials, from all sources, will be considered in light of this document and in relation to the overall instructional and educational purposes of the college.

General Priorities and Guidelines

Materials needed to support the current teaching programs of the college are of primary importance. Obviously, they should have a level of maturity appropriate to the needs of the students and faculty. Also vital are basic reference works and tools not directly related to any one college program, but which are of such importance that they belong in every academic library. The library collections should help to sustain cooperative or continuing education programs.

In addition, the library must provide the various print and other materials required to support the research of the faculty, and to assist the administration in the effective performance of their duties. Clearly, the library will not always be able to meet every research need with materials on hand, but library resources should be sufficient to aid in the preparation of lectures and other teaching activities. Interlibrary lending or individual purchases ought to be used for highly specialized materials.

To supplement the college archival program, the library has an obligation to collect published materials relating to the history and development of the college, of the greater Wilkes-Barre metropolitan area, and of the region.

Though of secondary or peripheral interest, the library will also consider purchase of materials relating to the recreational needs of the college community, especially in areas covered by instructional programs, as well as materials which may contribute to the future programs of the college.

Types of Books
The library will purchase single copies of hardback books whenever possible. Paperbound books will be acquired only when there is no choice in the format of binding, or when it is deemed necessary to purchase more than one copy for such short-term purposes as a special seminar or continuing education program.

Normally, textbooks will not be purchased. However, exceptions will be made when textbooks are considered classics by experts in the field, when other kinds of monographic publications in a curricular area are sparse, or when textbooks treat important areas not otherwise represented in the collection.

Books will be purchased primarily in the English language, except when foreign language titles are needed for language instruction and teaching, or for reference and other basic information considered necessary by faculty members in consultation with appropriate library personnel.

The library cannot normally acquire out-of-print books. However, if discontinued or antiquarian books are readily available from antiquarian book dealers or other sources, and there is a demonstrated need for such materials and sufficient funding available, the library will attempt to purchase them.

90

The library will purchase current fiction when it is of sufficient literary merit and contributes to the overall enrichment of the library collection. With the proximity of the Osterhout Public Library, there is little justification for routine expenditure of limited library funds for popular fiction. However, efforts will be made to provide a balanced and representative selection of the worlds's major literary figures, along with the supporting biographical and critical studies.

Serials

Serials are the major source of current information in a number of disciplines. Whether known as "periodicals," "journals," "magazines" or "newspapers," serials serve to keep the collection up-to-date, provide material not available in books and otherwise supplement the print collections. Some serials evaluate and review books, other serials, microforms, and non-print materials. The library establishes and maintains serial subscriptions with great care, since they are usually expensive long-term commitments. Subscriptions cannot be instituted casually. Any recommendations for the placement of new serial subscriptions must be made with a recognition of the peculiar nature of this format. The library must make the commitment to continue subscriptions indefinitely and to house the ever increasing backfiles of issues, whether in paper or microformat.

Selection criteria for serials include: indexing or abstracting in the appropriate reference sources, local availability, demonstrated need, scholarly reputation, and price. Subscriptions are made on a year-to-year basis and are charged to the library periodicals account. The library will continue to discourage the practice of charging serial subscriptions to departmental book budgets, though in exceptional cases temporary arrangements of this sort have been made. When a new journal subscription is deemed necessary, the appropriate academic department, in consultation with the library staff, may determine that another subscription or subscriptions in their discipline should be cancelled in order to free up limited funds. The preferable way to handle required additional subscriptions, particularly in new academic programs, is to build the projected cost of such journals into the college budget for the next fiscal year.

Due to the high cost and considerable space requirements for housing them, paper backfiles of serials cannot usually be purchased retrospectively. If sufficient demand for back issues of a journal develops, the library will attempt to acquire them in microformat.

Other Formats and Media

Besides current runs and backfiles of periodicals, the acquisition of materials in microform is limited normally to documents and special collections, such as ERIC and CIS (which may be available in that format only) and out-of-print books and titles which are too costly for purchase in their original form. Though no single microformat is preferred over another, selection is based on clarity of copy, availability of proper reader/printer hardware, relative ease of reproduction or copying, and types of format for similar materials already in the collection.

The library also allocates funds to academic departments for the rental and purchase of motion pictures, video and audio cassettes, slides, maps, software and various non-print materials Such media are selected with the same care as print materials. Most non-print materials, excluding microforms, are housed in the media center.

Gifts

The library accepts and acknowledges monetary gifts to subsidize the purchase of pertinent library materials. The library also receives gifts in kind and donations of books and other materials for its collections, using the same criteria for selection as regulary purchased items. All accepted gifts should fit into the definitions of relevant materials under the acquisitions policy and should generally have no restrictions attached to them. The library may refuse any gift which does not contribute to the mission and purpose of the library. The library staff will decide on the best disposition of gifts, including the location, classification, and circulation or non-circulation of such items. The library will not officially appraise books and other materials, or collections of such items, for tax or other purposes. The library does provide donors with a statement listing the amount of their monetary gift or, in the case of gifts in kind, the number of titles or items given. Detailed inventories are not usually possible. The library assumes no responsibility for the use donors make of such acknowledgements.

The library always retains the right to dispose of duplicates and any other unneeded materials as it deems appropriate. Disposal may be by direct sale, by gifts to other libraries, by discard, or other appropriate means.

Replacements, Weeding and Remote Storage

Library materials reported missing are not replaced automatically. Instead, potential replacements are evaluated using the same criteria for selection as regulary purchased items. Heavily used materials, determined to be necessary for teaching or research, will be replaced as quickly as possible if they are still available. However, some caution must be exercised in replacing costly items since experience shows that supposedly lost materials are often only temporarily missing. Such materials can be replaced as funding allows. If after five (5) years an individual bibliographic item is still missing and cannnot or will not be replaced, it is to be considered permanently lost and all records of it should be withdrawn from the shelf list, other catalogs, and databases.

De-accessioning, or "weeding," is an essential, on-going library routine, in which unneeded materials are removed permanently from the library collection. It is fundamentally different from transferring items to remote storage from a circulating collection. Examples of unneeded materials which might be targeted for withdrawal could include multiple copies, badly damaged or deteriorated books, out-of-date or chronically unused materials, broken runs of dated periodicals, and obsolete media materials. Remote storage is the preferred treatment for such items. However, the library staff members must reserve the right to de-accession library materials when, in their professional judgement, such a course of action is necessary because of a shortage of storage space or other serious constraints. Whenever possible, faculty members and other subject specialists should be invited to participate in the weeding process to assure that materials of historical or research interest are not inadvertently removed.

In periodically reviewing and evaluating the balance and strength of the collection the library staff may use standard bibliographies such as *Books for College Libraries* or those that appear in *Choice* and other appropriate sources.

Intellectual Freedom
The staff of the library supports the concept of intellectual freedom. As long as they fit into the general collection parameters of the library, all points of view and subjects will be considered without prejudice or censorship when determining the balance of the collection.

Revised: 28 February 1986

COLLECTION DEVELOPMENT POLICY
Part II

LEVELS OF COLLECTION DEVELOPMENT

It is a given that requirements for library materials will vary with different disciplines and subject areas. Specific requirements have been spelled out for each department in the following pages (not necessarily in order of priority), and four hierarchial levels of development have been identified:

Level 1. Minimum development. Subject areas which are outside the scope of the College curricula and in which there is little interest or activity. For example, because Wilkes has no programs in Hotel Management, the library should not have a large number of titles in the subject.

Level 2. Basic development. Materials which support the Core curriculum in all disciplines and/or all 100-numbered courses. This level should include surveys of the subject, introductory works, encyclopedias and handbooks, selected texts and the basic periodicals for the discipline.

Level 3. Intermediate development. This level supports all 200- and 300-numbered courses necessary for the undergraduate degree. Materials acquired should provide extensive coverage of all aspects of a discipline, and should support course work and independent undergraduate research. In addition to standard works and histories, purchases should include bibliographies and the major journals. Level 3 is built on Level 2.

Level 4. Advanced development. Herein are included those materials suitable for research and all graduate programs: primary source materials for each discipline, in-depth collecting of major authors and works (in original languages where appropriate), critical and analytical studies, emphasis on specific periods, subdivisions, or eras as required by the discipline, and the appropriate support journals.

Wilkes College
Wilkes Barre, Pennsylvania

College of Arts & Sciences

DEPARTMENT OF AEROSPACE STUDIES

Air Force ROTC participates with Wilkes College in a program to prepare students for commissions in the United States Air Force. While many of the teaching aids are supplied by the government, *e.g.* aeronautical history; tactics; aircraft maintenance and training, other materials are purchased for the Farley Library out of departmental funds.

Level 1:   Historical development of U.S. air power; textbooks; study guides; programmed instruction.

Level 2:   Management leadership practices; communicative skills; national defense policy; military tactics; pilot training; aircraft maintenance.
» Audio-visual materials «

Level 3:   Biographies (past & present) of leaders in military history, U.S. Presidents, and key civilians involved in national defense; new developments in the field.
» Audio-visual materials «

Level 4:   There is no graduate program.

Rev: 2/87

Wilkes College
Wilkes Barre, Pennsylvania

College of Arts & Sciences

DEPARTMENT OF ART

The Department of Art offers courses providing a broad foundation in art and other areas of study leading to the B.A. degree. The B.F.A. program requires more intensive study in a student's preferred art discipline. Areas of concentration include painting, sculpture, photography, print making, textile and commercial design. The library will attempt to purchase works of high quality in both color and black and white, recognizing that art students depend to a large degree upon good reproductions in their study of art history and techniques. The library should collect various media in all major art fields, as well as the principal artistic movements which have proved important to the development of Western art. Slides and other visual materials are generally the responsibility of the Department itself.

Level 1:   Collections and histories of non-Western art; biblioghraphies.

Level 2:   Minor media in painting and sculpture; textile design (batik, fiber, etc.); ceramics; biographies of artists.

Level 3:   History of Western art; painting in all major media (oil, acrylic, tempera, etc.); photography; printmaking (relief, intaglio, planographic); stone, wood, metal, plaster, and clay sculpture; drawing; graphic design.

Level 4:   There is no graduate program.

Rev: 2/87

Wilkes College
Wilkes Barre, Pennsylvania

College of Arts & Sciences

DEPARTMENT OF BIOLOGY

The Biology Department offers a general program in the basic areas of biology intended for those who plan to teach, enter the professional job market, or continue with graduate study.   The library should purchase materials in the basic structure and function of both plant life and animal life while also stressing those areas pertinent to the advanced and graduate programs.   High priority should be given to congresses and conference proceedings are to be given,   as well as to works of well-known and reputable authors of biological literature.

Level 1:   Animal behavior; marine biology; biographies.

Level 2:   Representative textbooks; selected classics in the biological sciences and modern biology; study guides and laboratory manuals; bibliographies.
            » Audio-visual materials «

Level 3:   Directories of individuals, foundations, research centers, and professional associations;   botany; invertebrate and developmental biology; evolution; bacteriology; ecology; microbiology; limnology; comparative anatomy, human anatomy, and physiology.
            Areas to be developed: Genetics, comparative physiology,   cellular biology, molecular biolgy.
            » Audio-visual materials «

Level 4:   Vertebrates; analytical cytology; parasitology; plant diversity; genetic toxicology.
            Areas to be developed: Immunology; molecular biology.
            » Software programs for instructional use «

Rev: 2/87

Wilkes College
Wilkes Barre, Pennsylvania

College of Arts & Sciences

DEPARTMENT OF CHEMISTRY

Courses in the Chemistry Department lead toward either the B.S. or B.A. degree. The curriculum is designed to provide a comprehensive background in the chemical sciences and equip students for careers in the health professions, engineering, or education. Since it is important that basic principles be grasped in the freshman and sophomore years so that they can be applied in the junior and senior years, selection of library titles is directed toward Levels 2 and 3, with the following broad areas supported: general chemistry; analytic, inorganic, and organic chemistry; physical and nuclear chemistry; biochemistry. Graduate level courses are aimed at degrees in chemical education.

The Department relies on recommended book lists, as well as meetings and symposia of the American Chemical Society to enhance the collection. Handbooks and texts are valuable and should be purchased on a regular basis, albeit with careful selection among available titles. Information retrieval, done either electronically or manually, is emphasized as part of the students' learning process, particularly in the history and literature of chemistry. Currency of material is vital; older titles should be weeded on a continuing basis.

Level 1: Peripheral areas of chemistry; biographies; bibliographies.

Level 2: Alchemy; physical and theoretical chemistry (except quantum); organic chemistry; techniques and operations; selected texts and handbooks.

Level 3: History of chemistry; research, study, and teaching; chemical analysis, especially qualitative and quantitative; inorganic chemistry; organic analysis and polymers; quantum chemistry; crystallography.

Level 4: Analytical, inorganic, organic, and physical chemistry beyond Level 3.

Rev: 2/87

College of Arts & Sciences

DEPARTMENT OF EDUCATION

The Department of Education offers a wide variety of courses on the undergraduate level to train students as teachers. On the graduate level courses in instructional methodology and educational curricula of pre-school, kindergarten, elementary, and secondary education enable practicing teachers to enhance their teaching skills. Materials related to these topics are vital to the livelihood of the program. The ERIC microfiche collection provides up-to-date information on all aspects of the education field and is a key resource for students in the discipline.

Level 1: Higher education; biographies; bibliographies.

Level 2: Special forms of education, such as adult education and private education; guidance; moral education;educational administration; surveys and reports ofcommissions and task forces.

Level 3: Children's literature; reading instruction and literacy; educational psychology and philosophy; history of education; school discipline; hygiene; educational games; educational measurements; media; innovations and technology; education of gifted and exceptional children, minorities and women; public education; urban education; educational planning; legislation affecting education.
Areas to be developed: Science education, educational computing, and speech pathology.

Level 4: Education and training of teachers. Graduate level courses in History and Literature are offered as a part of the Education master's degree.

Rev: 2/87

Wilkes College
Wilkes Barre, Pennsylvania

College of Arts & Sciences

DEPARTMENT OF HISTORY & POLITICAL SCIENCE

Courses given by the Department examine past and present economic, social, political, scientific, and religious conditions. Older, classical material is required for research but more emphasis should be placed on modern trends and conditions in history, politics, and government. The works of well-known and reputable historians and political scientists should be integral to the collection.

Level 1:   Africa, and Australasia; textbooks and study guides; directories; symposia and conference proceedings.

Level 2:   World civilization; United States history; concepts and methods in political science and American politics; public finance and administration. » Programmed learning materials and software for instructional use «

Level 3:   Ancient history; historiography and research; U.S. history from the
History   Colonial Period to the present; history of Western Europe, modern India, and the Far East.
              Areas to be developed: Eastern Europe, Near East, Latin America; modern China and Chinese Communism; history of Russia; French Revolution and Napoleon.

Level 3:   American Presidency and American political thought;
Political   communist systems.
Science   Areas to be developed: Comparative politics; government budgeting; democratic systems; international relations; Constitutional law; judicial process and policy; U.S. foreign policy; public adminsitration and local government; urban development, history, and planning.
              • Government documents and reports •

Level 4:   The graduate program is offered as part of the Education master's degree. Library materials beyond Level 3 in all subject areas should be purchased.

Rev: 2/87

College of Arts & Sciences

DEPARTMENT OF LANGUAGE AND LITERATURE

The Department offers a variety of programs for students interested in languages, the language arts, and literature. Majors are given in French, German, and Spanish language, as well as English language and literature. The predominence of courses are in English or American literature, but foreign language materials should be sufficient to support language study courses. The library should attempt to buy, whenever possible, quality works in the field of literature, as well as the interpretative and bibliographic material which supports these works. The library collection should also reflect the contributions of non-English writers to the body of world literature by purchasing English-language translations of representative and classic literature.

Level 1: Foreign literature in the original language; non-English vocabularies and grammars; current popular fiction.

Level 2: Anthologies of literature in English, primarily of the American and English literary tradition; grammars and language-building aids; style manuals; biographies; linguistics; writing; foreign literatures in translation (especially French, German, Italian, Russian, and Spanish), together with criticism and interpretation of foreign writers.

Level 3: English literature and American literature from their beginnings; criticism and interpretation of major writers and their works; bibliographies.

Level 4: The graduate program is offered as part of the Education master's degree. Library materials beyond Level 3 in all subject areas should be purchased.

Rev: 2/87

Wilkes College
Wilkes Barre, Pennsylvania

College of Arts & Sciences

DEPARTMENT OF MATHEMATICS / COMPUTER SCIENCE

A broad program of study in mathematics, statistics, and computer science is offered by the Department of Mathemtics/Computer Science. The library should attempt to collect in those areas which are emphasized by the curriculum. In general, only English-language versions of basic texts and classics in the field are sought. Recency of publication is extremely important for publications in computer science areas.

Level 1:   History, philosophy, and theory of mathematics; computer security; artificial intelligence; directories; laboratory manuals; foreign language publications.

Level 2:   Precalculus and calculus; classic texts of mathematics in English translation; congresses, symposia, andconference proceedings; bibliographies.
» Audio-visual materials «

Level 3:   Statistics; linear and differential algebra; set theory and logic; geometry; linear programming; operations research; biographies.
» Programmed learning materials and software for instructional use «

Level 4:   Abstract algebra; real and complex variables; topology.

Rev: 2/87

Wilkes College
Wilkes Barre, Pennsylvania

College of Arts & Sciences

DEPARTMENT OF MUSIC

The Department of Music has designed a program stressing musianship and educational skills. Students may receive degrees in applied performance or graduate with certification in music education (K-12). In a separate building from the Farley Library, the department maintains its own library of recordings and scores. As a result, the Farley Library is left to build in other areas of the discipline. Courses at the 300 level treat the teaching of music almost exclusively, with the material thereunto more logically collected within the perameters of the Education Department.

Level 1: Instrumental and vocal scores; librettos; philosophy and theory of music; acoustics and physics of music; bibliographies.

Level 2: Biographies; history and criticism; dictionaries and encyclopedias of music; instruction and study (composition, orchestration, voice training, instrumental techniques); analytical guides.

Level 3: Teaching of music.

Level 4: There is no graduate program.

Rev: 2/87

Wilkes College
Wilkes Barre, Pennsylvania

College of Arts & Sciences

DEPARTMENT OF NURSING

Professional nursing is built upon the integration of knowledge from the humanities, the physical and social sciences, nursing theories, and research.   The curriculum at Wilkes is based on the development of the individual throughout the life cycle.   Clinical resources at cooperating hospitals provide part of each student's training, with clinical performance an essential component of each course.   Currency is crucial in this program; therefore, dependence on journals, indexes, and books reflecting contemporary technique is essential.   The Nursing Laboratory has a small library of print and media publications, but it is the role of the Farley Library to provide in-depth resource material.

Level 1:   Directories;   foreign language publications;   programmed learning texts; popular works on health, diet, etc.

Level 2:   Basic texts and classics of nursing literature; laboratory manuals; biographies; bibliographies.
» Software programs for instructional use «

Level 3:   Nutrition; health care; care of youth and aged; pharmacology; research in nursing and contemporary issues; symposia and congress proceedings.
» Audio-visual materials «

Level 4:   There is no graduate program.

Rev: 2/87

Wilkes College
Wilkes Barre, Pennsylvania

College of Arts & Sciences

DEPARTMENT OF PHILOSOPHY

The Philosophy Department offers the B.A. degree with a major in philosophy. Traditional areas, such as ancient and medieval philosophy, logic, ethics, and metaphysics are covered, as well as general topics of modern and American philosophy. Emphasis is on material in English, although some effort is made to purchase works in their original languages. Contemporary translations and interpretations of standard works are important to the collection. The Department prefers titles which analyze or explain philosophical questions and the development of ideas. Authority, clarity of presentation, and permanence are important criteria.

Courses in religion are secondary, primarily because of Wilkes's proximity to King's College and College Misericordia, both religious-based institutions with strong collections to which Wilkes students have access. The Department offers courses in Old and New Testament, philosophy of religion, and contemporary religious thought, always stressing the importance of basic beliefs and how they have affected current events.

Level 1:	Oriental philosophy; modern philosophy of areas other than the United States and Europe; theology.
Level 2: **Philosophy**	Alexandrian, early Christian, medieval, and Renaissance philosophy; epistemology; ontology; cosmology; general works on ethics.
Level 2: **Religion**	History of Islam and Judaism; practical religion; works on specific denominations, *e.g.* Eastern Church, Orthodox Eastern Church, Protestantism, and Roman Catholic Church.
Level 3: **Philosophy**	History and systems of philosophy, especially of Greece and Rome; modern philosophy in the United States and Europe; logic;metaphysic; ethics.
Level 3: **Religion**	Religions of the world; Christianity; the Bible.
Level 4:	There is no graduate program.

Rev: 2/87

Wilkes College
Wilkes Barre, Pennsylvania

College of Arts & Sciences

DEPARTMENT OF PHYSICAL EDUCATION & HEALTH

The Department emphasizes participation in physical activity for self improvement, relaxation, and health. Most courses are non-credit.

Level 1:   History of sports; rules and regulations of games; biographies; bibliographies; sports stories and anthologies; periodicals.

Level 2:   Hygiene; sports played at the College: baseball, football, soccer, field hockey, golf, skiing, swimming; net sports such as badminton, tennis, etc.; aerobics; weight training.

Level 3:   Health, first aid, and sports medicine.

Level 4:   There is no graduate program.

Rev: 2/87

Wilkes College
Wilkes Barre, Pennsylvania

College of Arts & Sciences

DEPARTMENT OF PSYCHOLOGY

Courses in the Department of Psychology are designed to provide a basic understanding of the entire field of psychology. Core courses are spelled out with appropriate recommendations for those planning graduate work. Currency is important and materials which enhance a student's research capabilities are preferred.

Level 1:   Anthologies; foreign language materials; laboratory manuals; historical texts; biographies.

Level 2:   Basic and classic texts (in English); directories and other reference works; general psychology; symposia; history of psychology; human behavior; contemporary theories; testing; social, industrial, and comparative psychology.

Level 3:   Experimental, physiological, developmental, clinical and abnormal psychology; research topics.
» Audio-visual materials «

Level 4:   There is no graduate program.

Rev: 2/87

107

Wilkes College
Wilkes Barre, Pennsylvania

College of Arts & Sciences

DEPARTMENT OF SOCIOLOGY & ANTHROPOLOGY

The Sociology & Anthropology Department at Wilkes offers undergraduate courses which not only provide students with training for related careers, but also prepares students to better understand the society in which they live. For this reason, the subjects pertinent to the field include not only highly specialized interests (*e.g.* medical sociology), but also materials on contemporary issues, such as drug abuse and sexuality. Monographs and periodicals are the primary resources for this program, but audio-visual materials are a frequent, valuable supplement for the learning experience.

Level 1:   Anarchism; utoipias; socialism; communism.

Level 2:   Rural and urban groups; social welfare and comparative social welfare; cultural history; social history and reform; sexuality; feminism.

Level 3:   Archeology; anthropology; social problems, especially family violence, drug abuse, and alcoholism; criminology; penalogy; methods of research; social psychology; minorities; the family; area studies, particularly Middle East, Africa, and North American Indians.

Level 4:   There is no graduate program.

Rev: 2/87

108

College of Arts & Sciences

DEPARTMENT OF SPEECH, COMMUNICATION, & THEATER ARTS

Concentrations for the department are in rhetoric, public communication, interpersonal and organizational communication, broadcasting, journalism, and theater arts. The library must purchase materials which support not only these courses, but also those which contribute to the extracurricular college activities intimately connected with the discipline, such as the Debate Club, the *Beacon*, the radio station (WCLH), and the dramatic performances presented by the college.

Level 1:   Communication careers; communication theory.

Level 2:   History of journalism, radio, and television; interpersonal communication; diction; communication research methods.

Level 3:   Public speaking; argumentation and debate; persuasion; public relations; organizational communication; history of theater; theater production; American and world drama; newswriting; newspaper layout and design; editorial and feature writing; video production; acting and directing; communication law.

Level 4:   There is no graduate program.

Rev: 2/87

Wilkes College
Wilkes Barre, Pennsylvania

SCHOOL OF BUSINESS & ECONOMICS

DEPARTMENT OF COMMERCE & FINANCE

Majors are offered in accounting, business administration, and economics; graduate degrees are offered in accounting, finance, labor, managerial science and marketing. Emphasis is given to current and statistical material over historical, although certain basic classics are acknowledged. Only English language materials are purchased.

Level 1: Foreign aid; office computing.

Level 2: Demographics; credit; real estate; office management.

Level 3: History and theory of economics; international trade and investment; personnel management; business law; consumer behavior; statistics; taxation.

Level 4: Accounting and auditing; business administration and management; comparative economic systems; economic geography; government and business relations; industrial relations; labor and labor movements; collective bargaining; macro/micro theory; marketing; advertising; retailing; sales theory; money and banking; stocks and bonds; public finance; investing.

Rev: 2/87

Wilkes College
Wilkes Barre, Pennsylvania

SCHOOL OF BUSINESS & ECONOMICS

GRADUATE PROGRAM IN HEALTH SERVICE ADMINISTRATION

The Health Service Administration offerings are graduate-level programs intended to provide opportunities for specialization in management and decision-making in the health care industries and related fields. The program is transdisciplinary in design but coordinated from within the School of Business & Economics. Besides business subjects such as accounting, finance, marketing, and operations management, the curriculum provides opportunities for exploration into other academic areas.

Levels 1-4.　Most materials for this program will be purchased within the perameters of other disciplines, e.g., School of Business for all management, financial, and accountingsubjects; Department of Nursing for health-related areas; Department of Sociology & Anthropology for elements of social perspective and community relevence. The Library should maintain its current strengths in the undergraduate departments listed above. Other materials are very course-specific and will be ordered as needed.

Rev: 2/87

Wilkes College
Wilkes Barre, Pennsylvania

SCHOOL OF ENGINEERING & PHYSICAL SCIENCES

DEPARTMENT OF EARTH & ENVIRONMENTAL SCIENCES

The Department of Earth & Environmental Sciences is inter-disciplinary in nature. A strong background in all the sciences, as well as laboratory and field experience, provides the student with unique breadth of understanding of the principles and concepts of earth and environmental sciences, while emphasizing methods of analysis and experimentation. Courses require not only studies in the natural sciences but also in the social and political sciences. This department will draw upon the library's collection in many areas, so that collection development must be considered in relation to collection plans in other disciplines. Currency of material is important, but some historical perspective is necessary, especially in the humanities and social sciences.

Level 1: World physical geography; limnology; foreign language publications.

Level 2: Surveys--geologic, oceanographic, and meteorologic; field study; basic texts; directories; laboratory manuals; symposia and congress proceedings; bibliographies.

Level 3: Hazardous and solid waste management; hydrology; water quality and air quality measurement; geology; climatology; petrology; synoptic meteorology; mineralogy; geomorphology; ocean sciences; principles of environmental science.

Level 4: Materials suitable for advanced research and seminars with emphasis on field study, independent research, and professional off-campus experience.

Rev: 2/87

112

SCHOOL OF ENGINEERING & PHYSICAL SCIENCES

DEPARTMENT OF ENGINEERING

The Department of Engineering offers four-year programs in electrical, environmental, and materials engineering, as well as engineering management. There are also two-year offerings in various fields of specialization, *e.g.* aeronautical, chemical, civil, industrial, and mechanical engineering. A five-year B.S. engineering program is offered with liberal studies requirements as part of each semester's course of study, thereby providing a broad education in the arts and sciences. Currency is paramount, with periodicals and society publications considered especially important. The Library should hold recent titles in general engineering, basic computer and solid state electronics technologies, and the proceedings of conferences and symposia. Representative journals in all areas are required.

Level 1: Programmed learning texts and software; present strengths should be maintained in peripheral areas.

Level 2: General engineering topics, especially electrical, material, and materials science engineering; historical texts; directories; biographies; bibliographies.

> Audio-visual materials «

Level 3: Basic programming; computer architecture; microcomputer operation; solid state devices; control systems; ; electric machines; logic and switching circuitsand circuit theory; communication, especially microwave and antenna systems; energy management engineering; project and systems management; medical instrumentation; ceramics; polymers; mechanical and physical metallurgy; electrochemistry; X-ray diffraction; laboratory manuals; classic texts; English language materials published outside the United States, and foreign language publications in translation.

Level 4: Materials suitable for independent research and advanced seminars; periodicals and society publications, together with congress and symposia proceedings.

SCHOOL OF ENGINEERING & PHYSICAL SCIENCES

DEPARTMENT OF PHYSICS

The Department of Physics offers both the B.A. and B.S. degrees which enable students to continue with graduate study or enter the professional job market. The B.S. degree in Medical and Health Physics is also offered for undergraduates interested in these areas of health science. The library should attempt to keep abreast of modern physics theory and knowledge, since the discipline is steadily pushing back the boundaries of science. Proceedings and symposia are important acquisitions.

Level 1:   General physics texts; programmed learning materials.

Level 2:   Basic and historical texts in physics and the physical sciences, especially materials science and solid state physics; bibliographies; biographies; laboratory manuals. » Audio-visual materials and software programs for instructional use «

Level 3:   Astronomy; optics; light; electricity; magnetism; atomic, quantum, and nuclear physics; statics and dynamics; fluid mechanics; synoptic meteorology; mechanics; thermodynamics; society publications; congresses and symposia; directories; the works of reputable authors in the field, as well as English translations of important foreign-language publications.

Level 4:   Materials suitable for advanced research and seminars; advanced quantum mechanics; electrodynamics; nuclear processes and applications.

Rev: 2/87

POLICIES FOR SPECIAL COLLECTIONS - EXCERPTS

Concordia College
Moorhead, Minnesota

Philosophy Department -- Acquisitions Policy *1987*

Philosophy Department Goal

The Philosophy Department strives to assist students to develop skills of rational and systematic inquiry. These skills are developed by investigating philosophic ideas and movements in Western intellectual history and realizing the implications of those ideas as they apply to the cultural situations of our time. Emphasis is placed upon ancient Greek history and thought, modern European philosophy (with primary attention given to Descartes, Mume, and Kant), Existentialism (particularly Kierkegaardian and Sartrian thought) and philosophies of science, aesthetics, language and law. Other areas of particular interest are problems of epistemological and metaphysical character, and the investigation of the nature of ethical and religious belief.

Library Acquisitions Goal

The library will collect in the areas outlined in the department's goal -- i.e., philosophic ideas and movements in Western intellectual history with emphasis on ancient Greek history and thought; modern European philosophy, especially Descartes, Mume, and Kant; existentialism, particularly Kierkegaard and Sartre; philosophies of science, aesthetics, language and law; epistemological and metaphysical problems; and the nature of ethical and religious belief. Since philosophy is one of Concordia's Tri-College University responsibilities, collection development will be adequate to support advanced undergraduate or master's degree programs or sustained independent study (advanced study level as defined by the American Library Association Collection Development Committee).

Languages

With rare exceptions (Kierkegaard being one), language will be limited to works in English in accord with the library's overall Selection and Acquisitions Policy Statement: "The language departments are responsible for purchase of foreign-language materials, which shall be limited to those directly related to the language instructional program and accessible to the students' reading proficiency in the foreign language."

Other Limitations

None.

Types of Material Collected

Relevant printed materials preferably in hard copy, but microform is not excluded nor are audio-visual materials: slides, films, filmstrips, cassettes, videocassettes. Relevancy is defined as follows: primarily current as opposed to out-of-print monographs; general and advanced reference works; special author collections; reprints and facsimile editions.

Types of Material Excluded

Photographs.

Concordia College
Moorhead, Minnesota

Subjects and Collecting Levels*

B 1-631	History of philosophy, ancient philosophy including Greek and Roman	C1
B 635-765	Alexandrian, early Christian, Medieval	C1
B 765-4695	Renaissance to modern philosophy	C1
BC	Logic	C1
BD	Speculative philosophy	C1
BH	Aesthetics	C1
BJ	Ethics	C1

* The C1 level of collecting within the following divisions from the Library of Congress classification schedules is defined by the Library of Congress Collection Development Committee as advanced study level: i.e., adequate to support advanced undergraduate or master's degree programs or sustained independent study.

Drew University
Madison, New Jersey
EDUCATION

Dewey Nos.: 370-

Level of Collecting: 4 (Basic)

General Purpose: The University does not offer courses or any programs in what
is usually termed "professional education." There is, however, a concentration
in Christian Education within the Master of Divinity program and about ten
courses are listed in the catalog in this field.* Some materials in education
are also important for cultural history. Finally, the collection in this field
supports Drew's need for materials about college teaching and university administration, for pedagogic methodology and institutional research.

Geographical Areas: Essentially restricted to the United States and English-
speaking areas.

Other Factors: Drew has a cooperative arrangmenet with the College of St. Elizabeth whereby Drew students may take education courses there. These would be
courses which Drew does not offer but which may be recommended for teaching certification. For materials pertinent to these courses, Drew students may use
the St. Elizabeth library and it appears unnecessary to duplicate much of the
material acquired there. The history of American Protestant religious education is connected with the subject of American church history and is a research
area.

   *See subject of Practical Theology

ETHICS

Dewey areas: 170's (philosophy); 241 (Christian ethics); 610.17 (formerly bio-
        medical ehtics); 180's & 190's (individual philosophers); 200's (in-
        dividual theologians and biblical ethics)*; 296.385 (ethics in Juda-
        ism); 297.5 (ethics in Islam); 294.35 (ethics in Indic religions).

   *See also under Religion and Society; Systematic Theology: Philosophy

Level of Collecting: 2 (research)

General Purpose and scope: The collections in ethics support undergraduate work
in philosophy and religion; theological studies; and graduate work in the areas
of Religion and Society, Ethics, and Ethics and Politics. Special emphases in
the collection are: political, business, and bio-medical ethics, Christian
ethics, and the ethical thought of major theologians, Biblical authors (e.g.,
Paul), and philosophers.

Languages: Much of the collecting for undergraduate study is in English; but
for the study of ethics at the graduate and professional theological level,
German, French, and Spanish language materials are also collected.

Geographical areas: No limit; stress is mainly on the West, however.

Chronological limitations: None, but major emphases are on the 19th and 20th
centuries, & especially on contemporary issues.

Other factors: The collections in this area are closely related to collections
in theology and philosophy (especially in Biblical studies and the thought of
major theologicans.) There is a special interest in the ethical content of
literature as a component of religion and literature and of literary studies.

Drew University
Madison, New Jersey

INDEX TABLE OF SUBJECT AREAS AND COLLECTING LEVELS

Drew University
Madison, New Jersey

HISTORY

Dewey numbers: 900's, 326

Level of Collecting: 3 (advanced); 2 (in some areas of church or religious
history)

General Purpose: The collections in history support work toward the B.A.,
related work in the M.A./Ph.D. program in nineteenth-century studies, and
Ph.D. work in a variety of subject areas. Undergraduate majors are required to do course work in both European and American history. Th're
are courses in ancient history, Russian history from 1700, and history of
science.

Languages: The B.A. program does not require proficiency in a foreign
language. Generally acquisitions will be restricted to English language
materials with the exception of original language editions of selected
major historians. Russian materials in translation only.

Geographical areas: Particular emphasis is given to the United States,
Great Britain, the Ancient World, Western Europe (especially Germany and
France) and Russia. For these regions, collection encompasses cultural,
social, political, and intellectual history. Collecting is more selective
for China, Africa, Latin America, and India, and is generally restricted
to major studies, and general ones.

Chronological Limitations: None

Other Factors: The Library has a strong collection of 19th-century
Afro-American slavery materials, especially slave narratives. Materials
which add depth and scope to this collection are considered for acquisition.
        History of science is another area of collection development
This collection supports both undergraduate course work and graduate courses
in the 19th-century studies program. The emphasis is on the development
of scientific ideas and their impact on social and intellectual history.
Some special interest in the development of evolutionary theory and its
relation to religious controversy.

See also the following subject descriptions:
    Church history
    Classics
    Near Eastern Archaeology

Drew University
Madison, New Jersey

(revised 7/84)

MATHEMATICS AND COMPUTER SCIENCE

Dewey numbers: 510's, 001.6

Collecting Level: 3

General Purpose and Scope: The collection supports work toward the B.A. degree and
a major in mathematics or computer science. Emphasis is in the following subject
areas: linear algebra, differential equations, advanced calculus, abstract algebra,
computer theory and computer applications.

Languages: Acquisitions restricted to English language materials.

Chronological limitations: Emphasis primarily on contemporary mathematics and
computer science.

Geographical restrictions: Not applicable.

Materials excluded: Most textbooks; audio-visual materials, curricular software.

Notes: Materials in mathematics and computer science may be chosen in support of
undergraduate course work in the sciences, social sciences and humanities:
statistics, probability theory, sampling and computer applications.

SCOPE NOTE   SCOPE NOTE   SCOPE NOTE

COMPUTER INITIATIVE

Beginning with the fall 1984 class, each entering freshman will be given a
personal computer. Computer use is to be integrated into the college curriculum. I
is expected that many graduate and theological school students will also purchase
computers. The Library does not purchase or maintain software collections; that
responsibility lies with the Academic Computing Center. The Library does support
faculty and student needs for monographs and journals that arise from the Computer
Initiative. These can include subscriptions to popular computing magazines,
computer-aided instructions books and basic computer science texts for faculty self-
instruction.

Drew University
Madison, New Jersey

SPANISH LANGUAGE AND LITERATURE

Dewey numbers: 460 860

Level of collecting: 3

Purpose: The collection supports work leading to the B.A. degree with
an emphasis either in Spanish literature or Spanish language and culture.

Languages Collected: Original works are collected in Spanish and in
English translation. Commentary is collected primarily in English and
occasionally in Spanish.

Geographical areas: Spain, and Spanish literature from Latin America
and the Caribbean.

Chronological limitations: Writings of and pertaining to major authors
in Spain from the Middle Ages to the present are collected. The emphasis
in collection of Spanish American literature is on the 20th century,
but works of significant earlier authors will be collected. Works
in Spanish surveying contemporary Spanish and Spanish American culture
and substantial critical or historical writings in Spanish dealing
with any period will be collected.

Types of material collected: Writings of major authors and specific
criticism relating to them. General criticism of periods, genres, or
literary groups. Studies of language appropriate to the language teaching
function. Reference works, including author and general literary
bibliographies, language dictionaries, atlases, handbooks, and major
encyclopedias. Periodicals relating to Spanish and Spanish American
literature and culture. Several general interest popular periodicals
may be acquired for reading practice associated with language courses.

HISTORY DEPARTMENT
Order Priorities for Library Acquisitions
November, 1987

	HEAVY	CONSIDERABLE	MEDIUM	LIGHT
United States				
Political - All periods	✓			
Social and Cultural	✓			
Labor	✓			
Economic and Business	✓			
Black History	✓			
Urban History	✓			
Southern History	✓			
Diplomacy and Foreign Policy	✓			
Ethnic and Minorities	✓			
Historiography - Methods	✓			
Ancient				
Greece	✓			
Rome	✓			
Europe				
General European Political				
Medieval	✓			
Renaissance/Reformation	✓			
500-1500 A.D.	✓			
1500-1800 A.D.	✓			
1800 to Present	✓			
General European Economic				
500-1500 A.D.	✓			
1500-1800 A.D.	✓			
1800 to Present	✓			
European Intellectual, 1500 to Present				
	✓			
National Histories				
England	✓			
France	✓			
Germany	✓			
Italy		✓		
Russia	✓			
Spain/Portugal		✓		
Other regions				
Hapsburg Empire	✓			
Balkans (20th century)	✓			
Other East Europe (20th century)	✓			
Benelux			✓	
Scandinavia			✓	
European historiography				
		✓		

HISTORY DEPARTMENT
Order Priorities for Library Acquisition (cont.)

	HEAVY	CONSIDERABLE	MEDIUM	LIGHT
Canada				
			✓	
Latin America/Caribbean				
			✓	
Africa				
Political				
West Africa			✓	
East Africa				✓
Arab Africa				✓
Social and cultural				
				✓
Asia				
South. Asia				
India	✓			
Pakistan	✓			
Bangladesh		✓		
Sri Lanka		✓		
Southeast Asia				
Burma		✓		
Thailand		✓		
Malaysia		✓		
Singapore		✓		
East Asia				
China	✓			
Japan	✓			
Korea	✓			
Taiwan		✓		
Hong Kong		✓		
History of Communism and Communist states				
	✓			
Women s History				
	✓			

South Carolina State College
Orangeburg, South Carolina

MILLER F. WHITTAKER LIBRARY

EDUCATIONAL ADMINISTRATION

Collection Development Policy

November, 1982

INTRODUCTION

The Educational Administration program at South Carolina State College
has three major objectives:

1. to prepare school administrators for effective educational
   leadership throughout the state.

2. to provide educational management services to school districts
   statewide.

3. to increase the academic offerings at the College as a means
   of attracting a more diverse student body to the campus.

The program encompasses two degree levels: Doctor of Education (Ed.D) and
Educational Specialist (Ed.S.)
       Selection of materials basic to this discipline is delegated to a Collection Develop-
ment Committee who will evaluate the present collection; consult approprate
bibliographies and make recommendation for purchase both independently and
in conjunction with the academic faculty.

TYPES OF MATERIALS

The collection should represent a qualitative selection of scholarly
materials appropriate for instructional, supplemental and independent research.
Included are current publications of research value, critical works, contemporary
pamphlets, published documents, proceedings, special agency reports, and retrospective publications.

Books

Major emphasis should be on selecting current publications; however,
retrospective purchases are qcquired for historical perspective.
       If a title has several editions, the most recent will be purchased unless
the earlier work contains information of historical value, of if it contains
materials excluded form the latest edition.

Periodicals

Multi-year periodical subscriptions are recommended with automatic renewal.
Relevant microfiche and microfilm publications will be purchased based on
availability and type of material. Backfiles of periodical titles and collections

South Carolina State College
Orangeburg, South Carolina

of materials used for basic research could be acquired in microform format.

Government Documents

As a partial federal-depository-library, selection of publications from the Office of Education, National Institute of Educational Statistics and other agencies are obtained from the Superintendent of Documents.

Indexes and Abstracting Services

Abstracts and indexes for bibliographic accessibility should be purchased to ensure access to literature in the field.

Dissertations

The library will acquire, in microfilm format, dissertations in the area of Educational Administration. Copies of South Carolina State College dissertations will be added to the collection upon availability.

Online Services

Subscription to on-line systems and services should be maintained to provide accessibility through various educational data-banks.

NON-SUBSCRIPTIVE MATERIALS

Textbooks

Purchase of textbooks should be kept at a minimum. Additions to the collection are made only when textbooks are recognized as the best source of informatio on a subject. If individual authors have written other books on the topic, then these titles will be ordered in lieu of requested textbooks.

Paperbacks

Books should be selected on the basis of content rather than format. Paperbacl are selected when they are the only format available.

Media

Requests for audio-visual materials are refered to the Instructional Media Center on campus.

Elizabeth Coates Maddux Library
Trinity University, San Antonio TX 78284
COLLECTION DEVELOPMENT STATEMENT

COLLECTING LEVELS

0. Out of Scope: The Library does not collect in this area.

1. Minimal Level: A subject area in which few selections are made beyond
    very basic or introductory works.

2. Basic Information Level: A collection of up-to-date general materials that
    serves to introduce and define a subject and to indicate the varieties of
    information available elsewhere. It may include dictionaries, encyclopedias,
    selected editions of important works, historical survey, bibliographies,
    handbooks and other reference tools, a few major periodicals, in the minimum
    number that will serve the purpose. While a basic information level collection
    is not sufficient to support an upper-level undergraduate course or independent
    study in the subject area involved, it is an adequate level to support lower
    level courses requiring little library use.

3a. Initial Study Level: A collection which is adequate to support undergraduate
    courses. It includes a judicious selection of both current and retrospective
    monographs; a broad selection of works of more important writers; a selection
    of major journals; and current editions of the most significant reference tools
    and bibliographies pertaining to the subject.

3b. Advanced Study Level: A collection which is adequate to support upper level,
    library oriented undergraduate courses; sustained independent study; and/or
    master's degree programs; that is, adequate to maintain knowledge of a subject
    required for limited or generalized purposes of less than research intensity.
    It includes a wide range of basic monographs both current and retrospective,
    complete collections of the works of more important writers, selections from
    the works of secondary writers, a collection of journals supporting faculty
    teaching interests and local curricular strengths as well as the various
    general aspects of the subject, and the reference tools and fundamental
    bibliographic apparatus pertaining to the subject.

4. Research Level: A collection which includes published source materials
    required for dissertations and sustained independent research. It contains
    all important reference works and a wide selection of specialized monographs,
    journals, technical and scholarly reports, and other materials reporting
    research. Older material is retained for historical research.

5. Exhaustive Level: A collection in which a library endeavors, so far as
    is reasonably possible, to include all relevant sorts of recorded knowledge,
    manuscripts (in all applicable languages) and ephemera. This level of
    collecting intensity is one that maintains a "special collection," the aim of
    which, if not the achievement, is a nationally recognized exhaustiveness.

Elizabeth Coates Maddux Library
Trinity University, San Antonio TX 78284
COLLECTION DEVELOPMENT STATEMENT

LANGUAGE CODES

E--English language predominates; little or no foreign language material in the collection.

F--English language predominates; foreign language primary-sources, reference works, and major secondary sources are selectively purchased to support specifically defined curricular strengths and faculty interests.

W--Wide selection of foreign language materials in all applicable languages.

Y--Material is primarily in one foreign language.

Elizabeth Coates Maddux Library
Trinity University, San Antonio TX 78284
COLLECTION DEVELOPMENT STATEMENT

ART HISTORY

Purpose of the Collection: To support undergraduate teaching and faculty
research in art history with a strong collection of scholarly resources
supported by key reference books, significant exhibition catalogues, and some
popular trade book titles. Students and faculty from other areas of humanistic
and fine arts studies will benefit from a strong art history collection.

General Collection Guideline

A. Languages: While English dominates, there are restrictions. Some
materials, often heavily illustrated titles in modern European, classical,
and Asian languages are acquired. Translations of scholarly works into
English are acquired, but many key texts will be acquired in original
languages.

B. Chronological Guidelines: No restrictions.

C. Geographical Guidelines: Areas of special interest are: Ancient
Mediterranean world, Medieval Europe and the Renaissance, Modern Europe to
the present including England, America to the present. Areas of lesser
interest are Asia and Latin America. The arts of Africa, Egypt, Western
Asia, and Oceana receive the least emphasis. Special faculty interests
outside the art history department include: Native American and
contemporary Southwestern art, Russian art of the 20th century, the art of
Latin America, and archaeology of the Holy Land including Egypt.

D. Treatment of Subject: Historical and critical studies of periods,
specific artists, and artistic media over several periods dominate the
collection. High quality trade book titles with notable illustrations are
acquired. Primary source compilations of documents and visual materials
are collected as are reference materials such as dictionaries, handbooks,
encyclopedias, biographical sources and directories, bibliographies, and
library catalogues.

E. Types of Materials: Monographs, exhibition catalogues, and serials
form the nucleus of the collection. Much of the material is heavily
illustrated. While miocroforms will be acquired when appropriate, this is
often an undesirable alternative if illustrations are an essential part of
the work. The same holds true for any reprint editions. Nonbook
materials other than slides are acquired to support specific course
objectives.

F. Date of Publication: No limitations. Retrospective collection
development is extremely important.

G. Other Factors for Consideration: The Art and Art History Departments
maintain a Slide Library.

H. Subject and Collection Levels:

   1. Ancient

      a. Egypt and Western Asia   2   F

      b. Classical World, including Crete, Mycenae, Greece,

          Etruria, Rome   3b   W

   2. Western Regions, excluding North America

a.	Medieval	3b	F
b.	Renaissancè	3b	W
c.	Baroque	3b	F
d.	Neoclassical	3b	F
e.	Romantic	3b	F
f.	Modern	3a	W

   3. The Americas

a.	North American Indian	2	E
b.	South American Indian (Mexico, Peru)	2	F
c.	United States	3a	E
d.	Latin America	2	F

   4. Oriental Countries

a.	China	2	F
b.	Japan	2	F
c.	India	2	E
d.	Other	1	F

   5. Islamic   1   F

   6. Primitive

a.	Africa	1	F
b.	Oceana	1	F

In all areas, the subjects covered include: painting, drawing, sculpture,
printmaking, and architecture. Of course, applied arts such as mosaics,
tapestries, metalwork, pottery and porcelain, glass, and jewelry are of
significance during specific periods. Costume is typically covered by
theater interests rather than art.

Elizabeth Coates Maddux Library
Trinity University, San Antonio TX 78284
COLLECTION DEVELOPMENT STATEMENT

BIOLOGY

Purpose of the Collection: To support undergraduate education in general
biology, with certain emphases which reflect faculty research interests.

General Collection Guidelines:

A. Languages: Almost-exclusively English. Some descriptive botanical
   material in Latin.

B. Chronological Guidelines: Not applicable.

C. Geographical Guidelines: Emphasis on flora and fauna materials will be
   Southwestern U.S. and subtropical Mexico. General works on other areas of
   the world are of interest, but not much in the way of specific area
   studies.

D. Treatment of Materials: Some small number of general biology
   textbooks, but most in the collection will come from faculty donations of
   review copies. On the whole, textbooks not an important part of the
   collection.

E. Format of Materials: Primarily, periodicals and monographs.

F. Date of Publication: Emphasize current, except for history of science
   materials.

G. Other Factors for Consideration: Pre-med aspect of biology major
   cannot be ignored; material on professions and employment in the medical
   biological sciences should be bought, but selectively. Health Science
   textbooks buying should be held to a minimum, but some occasionally placed
   in Reference. Any books dealing with clinical aspects of a disease or an
   organ should be looked upon with a healthy skepticism. In fact, almost any
   book dealing with disease should be treated so. General interest drug and
   pharmaceutical industry books are purchased, but books on specific drugs
   and drug treatments seldom are. Animal husbandry is not of interest. Go
   easy on the botany materials: very little taught, and what is taught is
   very general.

H. Subjects and Collecting Levels

   a. To support undergraduate curriculum:

      1. Cell biology   3a
      2. Ecology   3a
      3. History of Science   3a
      4. Microbiology   3a
      5. Regional Ecology   3a
      6. Zoology   3a
      7. Botany   3a

132

Trinity University
San Antonio, Texas

b. To reflect faculty research interests:

1. Cytology   3a
2. Cancer   3a
3. Endocrinology   3a
4. Immunology   3a
5. Poultry Physiology   3a

Elizabeth Coates Maddux Library
Trinity University, San Antonio TX 78284
COLLECTION DEVELOPMENT STATEMENT

ENGLISH

Purpose of the Collection: To support undergraduate teaching and faculty
research in English and American literature primarily, but also in other
literatures in the English language. Materials purchased include literary texts
in all genres, criticism, literary theory, literary history, biography,
folklore, rhetoric, linguistics, bibliography and research methodology.

General Collection Guidelines

A. Languages: English, obviously, is the primary language. Critical and
historical treatments will be acquired in other modern languages very
selectively. English translations of such works will be purchased when
available. Translations of literature in English into other languages are
not purchased, except in special, well-justified instances.

B. Chronological Guidelines: No limitations or special emphasis.

C. Geographical Guidelines: Literatures in English from the United States
and British Isles (Great Britain and Ireland) are emphasized. The
literatures of other countries, such as Australia, Canada and South
Africa, are collected at levels to support courses in the curriculum and
represent authors of international stature. Literary works from these
regions in languages other than English (e.g. Welsh, Spanish, Yiddish)
are purchased very selectively. With regard to language study and
linguistics only basic works on the history, development, and grammar of
languages other than those taught at Trinity University (English, Spanish,
French, Russian, German, Latin and Greek) will be purchased.

D. Treatment of Subject: Historical and critical treatments will be
purchased at the same level as the literatures and specific authors
themselves. Biographies of writers, critics and bibliographers will be
sought out. While all genres of literature are collected, special emphasis
is placed on fiction, drama, and poetry. Theoretical works are purchased
in all areas as well. Stylistic handbooks will be acquired selectively as
will guides to the marketing of literary production. Legal aspects of
copyright are also of interest. Popular treatments of literary subjects
are not normally acquired; however, creative works which are popular in the
sense of being widely read will be selectively acquired. Juvenilia by
major writers will be purchased. Children's and adolescent literature
generally is the responsibility of the Education Librarian. Anthologies
and readers analyzed by major reference tools will be acquired; rhetoric
textbooks intended for undergraduate instruction will not be ordered except
in special circumstances.

134

Trinity University
San Antonio, Texas

E. <u>Types of Materials</u>: Monographs and serials form the nucleus of the collection. A strong selection of critical journals is maintained; literary reviews are subscribed to only if major stature is attained. There is a recognized need for sound recordings of poetry and drama, video-recorded drama, and dramatizations of literary classics recorded on video which support classroom instruction.

F. <u>Date of Publication</u>: No limitations. In many instances, original editions are not necessary; reprints or microforms are appropriate. In linguistics, emphasis is on acquisition of current materials.

G. <u>Other General Consideration</u>: Students in literature in English will be interested in history and criticism of the arts as well as the history of ideas.

H. <u>Subjects and Collecting Levels</u>:

1. <u>United States</u>:

    a. Colonial and Formative Period (1606-1820)   3b E
    b. 1820-1920--Emphasis on Transcendentalist movement 3b E
       and on fiction, especially Melville and Twain:
       development of modernist poetry, especially Pound.
    c. 1920-Present--Emphasis on Faulkner, Hemingway, 3b E
       O'Neill: criticism of their works may need further
       development. Also emphasis on poetry since 1945.
    d. Beginnings to Present--Selected authors, literary 3b E
       movements, themes, genres, and literature of
       ethnic groups related to faculty research interests
       and course development.

2. <u>British Isles</u>:

    a. Anglo-Saxon period (ca. 600-1100): Emphasis 3a E
       on poetry.
    b. Middle English (1100-1500): Emphasis on poetry 3a E
       and romances.
    c. Renaissance to Restoration (1500-1660): Emphasis 3a E
       on poetry and drama.
    d. Restoration to Romantic Revival (1660-1800): 3a E
       Inclusion of Irish writers begins around this
       date. Emphasis on essayists, such as Johnson,
       Swift, Addison, etc.
    e. Nineteenth Century (1800-1900): Emphasis on 3a E
       Romantic movement, the novel, prose writers such
       as Arnold, Newman, Pater and Ruskin; and the
       beginning of the Irish Renaissance.
    f. Twentieth Century (1900-present): Emphasis 3a E
       on Irish Renaissance; modernist poetry, especially
       Eliot; and the period since 1945.
    g. Scotland: Literature in Scots, beginning ca. 1100, 1 E
       will be minimally represented. (Exception: Burns "C")

135

h. Beginnings to present--Selected authors, literary   3a   E
movements, themes, genres, and literature of ethnic
groups related to faculty research, interests and
course development.

3. Other English literatures, with works by and about authors   3a   E
of international stature, such as Margaret Atwood (Canada),
Patrick White (Australia), N.K. Narayan (India) and Nadine
Gordimer (South Africa).

4. Works Associated with the intellectual history of ideas.   3a   F

5. Linguistics

    a. English language   3a   E
    b. Sociolinguistics   3a   F
    c. Psycholinguistics   3a   E
    d. English as a second language   3a   F
    e. Other languages. Only basic books on the history,
    development and grammar of languages other than
    those taught at Trinity University (English, Spanish,
    French, Russian, German, Italian, Latin and Greek)
    will be purchased. There is, however, significant
    faculty interest in Asian and Near Eastern languages,
    such as Hebrew, Arabic, Sanskrit, Chinese and Japanese.
    There is also demonstrable faculty interest in Italian
    and Swedish. The former is of particular interest to
    the Music Department and History.   2   F

6. Rhetoric (theory of and teaching of)   3b   E

7. Critical Theory   3b   F

8. Mythology   3a   F

9. Folklore   2   F

10. Translations of significant literary works
from all languages into English are purchased
systematically through approval plans and other
acquisitions mechanisms.   3a   E

Elizabeth Coates Maddux Library
Trinity University, San Antonio TX 78284
COLLECTION DEVELOPMENT STATEMENT

GEOLOGY

Purpose of the Collection: To support an undergraduate geology program, and to serve as a partial research collection for undergraduate and faculty research projects.

General Collection Guidelines:

A. Languages: Primarily, collection will be in English, but some French and German.

B. Chronological Guidelines: Not applicable.

C. Geographical Guidelines: Heavy emphasis on the geology of Texas with somewhat selective collecting on New Mexico, Arizona, Utah, Colorado, Wyoming, Oklahoma, California, and the Gulf Coast states. General materials on North American geology, and selected titles on the general geology of other countries and continents.

D. Treatment of Materials: Not applicable.

E. Format of Materials: All print formats, with microforms substituting if necessary, but only if paper is not available. Government publications, especially those of:

> U.S. Bureau of Mines
> U.S. Geological Survey
> Texas Bureau of Geological Survey

Maps are vitally important, both from these agencies and from commercial publishers and societies. Field trip guidebooks and society publications are very important.

F. Date of Publication: Geology literature does not date. Emphasize current material, but important retrospective materials should be acquired, too.

G. Other Factors for Consideration: Much of the geological literature is found in the publications of geological societies. Therefore, approval plans are insufficient aids to collection in this field. A list of important societies has been identified by the Geology faculty for regular purchase of their published materials. List is attached.

H. Subjects and Collecting Levels:

A. To support undergraduate teaching:

1. Field geology   3a
2. Geochemistry   3a
3. Geomorphology   3a

Trinity University
San Antonio, Texas

        4. Geophysics   3a
        5. Glaciology   3a
        6. Historical geology   3a
        7. History of geology   3a
        8. Hydrology   3a
        9. Meteorology   3a
       10. Oceanography   3a
       11. Physical Geology   3a
       12. Seismology   3a

    B. A good basic collection:

        1. Economic geology   3a
        2. Petrology   3a
        3. Photogeology   3a
        4. Stratigraphy   3a
        5. X-ray analysis   3a

    C. To support faculty research interests:

        1. Crystallography   3a
        2. Invertebrate paleontology   3a
        3. Mineralogy   3a
        4. Optical mineralogy   3a
        5. Petrology   3a
        6. Petroleum geology   3a
        7. Sedimentology   3a
        8. Structural geology   3a
        9. Tectonics   3a
       10. Volcanology   3a

Elizabeth Coates Maddux Library
Trinity University, San Antonio TX 78284
COLLECTION DEVELOPMENT STATEMENT

HISTORY

<u>Purpose of the Collection</u>: To support undergraduate teaching and faculty
research in the discipline of history with a strong collection of primary
sources and secondary literature.

<u>General Collection Guidelines</u>:

A. <u>Languages</u>: The primary language is English. Some materials, both
primary and secondary, in other modern and classical languages are
acquired if in demand for specific teaching or research needs.
Translations of both primary and secondary sources into English are
also acquired whenever available.

B. <u>Chronological Guidelines</u>: No limitations, but the specific interests
of the department are reflected in the following: Ancient Greece and Rome,
Europe, Renaissance and Modern Europe including Great Britain, U.S. and
Latin American history - beginnings to the present, and Asia - early
history or modern.

C. <u>Geographical Guidelines</u>: Areas of special interest are: the Mediterranean
area, Europe, British Isles, North America and Latin America with special
emphasis on the South/Southwestern region of the U.S. and on Mexico and with
lesser emphasis on Canada, and Asia - with special emphasis on Malaysia,
India, China, Japan, and Korea. There is little interest in the Modern Near
East, Arabic World and Africa - early history or modern.

D. <u>Treatment of Subject</u>: Primary and secondary sources are purchased.
Biographies are viewed as especially important secondary resources.
Reference materials, such as dictionaries, handbooks, bibliographies and
multi-volume histories, are collected. Popular level materials are
selectively purchased if relevant as documents of social history.

E. <u>Types of Material</u>: Monographs and serials are the major types of
materials acquired. Microforms are acceptible if hard copy formats are not
available or too expensive. There is a definite interest in obtaining
microform collections of primary source materials (that could be otherwise
unavailable) which support teaching efforts. Theses and dissertations are
occasionally purchased to support teaching and research areas of emphasis.
Audio visual materials are selectively acquired to support specific
classroom teaching objectives.

F. <u>Date of Publication</u>: No limitations.

Trinity University
San Antonio, Texas

G. Subjects and Collecting Levels:

1. Ancient Greece and Rome   3b   F

2. Europe

   a. Pre-history   1   E
   b. Medieval World   3b   F
   c. Renaissance   3b   F
   d. Modern Europe   3b   F

3. United States, excluding pre-history   3b   E

   a. Pre-history   2   E

4. Other North America   2   E

5. Latin America

   a. Pre-history   2   E
   b. Mexico   3b   F
   c. Other, including Caribbean   3a   F

6. Asia

   a. Pre-history   1   E
   b. South Asia, especially India   3a   E
   c. Southeast Asia, especially Malaysia   3a   E
   d. China, Japan, and Korea   3a   E
   e. Other   1   E

7. Near East/Arab World, including Egypt

   a. Early history (Old-New Testament Period)   2   F
   b. Modern   1   E

8. Africa, excluding Egypt   1   E

9. Pacific Region, Arctic Region & Anarctica   1   E

140

Elizabeth Coates Maddux Library
Trinity University, San Antonio TX 78284
COLLECTION DEVELOPMENT STATEMENT

POLITICAL SCIENCE

Purpose of the Collection: To provide library resources for undergraduates in
Political Science courses and to provide support for faculty research and
teaching. The collection also provides support for students and faculty in
other departments who use public policy and legal resource materials.

General Collection Guidelines:

A. Languages: Primary emphasis is given to English language materials.
Spanish and Portuguese materials originating in Latin America will be
purchased as needed. Titles published in European languages may be
selectively acquired for some aspects of comparative government and
politics, political theory, comparative and international law, and
international relations. For the most part, works in foreign languages
will be purchased only in English translation.

B. Chronological Guidelines: Although there is an emphasis on contemporary
affairs, certain areas, such as comparative government and politics,
international relations, and political theory, will require materials
dealing with earlier periods. For English and American constitutional
history, materials from any period are relevant to existing course work.

C. Geographical Guidelines: There is a strong emphasis on American government
and politics from the national to the local level. Strong interests also
exist for Latin America, United Kingdom, the Commonwealth (primarily Canada,
Australia, India,) western Europe, eastern Europe, and the U.S.S.R. Books
and journals dealing with Asia and Africa will be selectively purchased.

D. Treatment of Subject: Biographies of political and legal figures are
collected extensively, especially those of national (or Texas) interest.
Upper level textbooks are occasionally purchased, as needed. We subscribe
to selected legal on-going sets such as codes, court reports, etc. Our
commitment in this area is restricted to: U.S. statutes, U.S. Supreme
Court reports, Texas statutes, and Texas court reports. Introductory
textbooks and books or periodicals categorized as "popular" are not
collected. We do attempt to add materials to this collection which
represent different political opinions and viewpoints.

E. Types of Materials: Most materials acquired will be books (including
numbered monographs) and periodicals. Society publications as well as
the translations and proceedings of conferences are purchased on a
selective basis. Doctoral dissertations are seldom purchased. Microforms
are also acceptable for primary source material (state papers, parliamentary
records, etc.) when hard copy is too expensive or unavailable. Microforms
are also acceptible for periodical backfiles. Audiovisual materials will
be purchased selectively as needed to support teaching and course-related
projects. The Political Science Department relies heavily on the depository

collections of U.S., Texas, and San Antonio documents. United Nations and other international documents as well as those issued by foreign governments are very selectively purchased. Corporate reports of transnational corporations are regularly acquired to support the course on "The Multinational Corporation in International Politics."

F. Date of Publication: Primary emphasis in on new materials. Currency is essential in order to support student research projects. Retrospective collection development efforts are also important, especially in the areas of American politics, political theory, and constitutional law and legal history.

G. Other Factors for Consideration: Primary interest in the quality of this library collection naturally resides in the Political Science Department. However, students and faculty elsewhere on campus have strong related interests. Social science methodology is of strong interest to sociologists, psychologists, urban planners, and economists, as well as to political scientists. Historians have overlapping interests in constitutional and political history. The collection also provides support for students, faculty, and staff on campus who use the public policy or legal resources. The students and faculty in the departments of Gerontology and Urban Studies share the political scientists' reliance on our government documents collection.

H. Subjects and Collecting Levels:

1. American government and public policy   3b
2. International politics/U.S. foreign policy   3b
3. Comparative government and politics:

    Western Europe, United Kingdom,
    Mexico, U.S.S.R., China   3b
    Other areas.   3a
4. Public law   3b
5. Political Theory   3a
6. Public administration   3a

POLICIES FOR SPECIAL COLLECTIONS

College of St. Thomas
St. Paul, Minnesota

DEPARTMENT OF SPECIAL COLLECTIONS

COLLECTION DEVELOPMENT STATEMENT

I. INTRODUCTION.

The purpose of this "Special" collection development
statement is to supplement the general statement which governs
the growth of the O'Shaughnessy Library's main collection by
outlining the criteria employed when acquiring material for the
Library's "Department of Special Collections."

The Department's current strengths and areas of development
are outlined below in a listing which follows the broad divisions
of the Library of Congress classification system also used in
delineating subject areas in the Collection Development Statement
for the general collection.

The materials which now constitute the Department's holdings
have grown form a number of different sources. The "Celtic
Collection," which constitutes the vast majority of the
Department's holdings, resulted from three major gifts to the
College: the Ancient Order of Hibernians gift of 1917, the Peter
O'Connor family gift of 1936, and the O'Toole Library gift of
1956.

Materials received in the Hibernian donation were books
published between roughly 1875 and 1917 which focused on then-
contemporary Irish history and politics. This collection
consisted of between 500 and 600 volumes. The materials in the
O'Connor donation, some 3,000 - 4,000 bound volumes (plus unbound
periodicals), were items published from 1496 to 1900.

145

College of St. Thomas
St. Paul, Minnesota

Approximately 530 of the O'Connor volumes were published before
1800. The O'Connor collection consisted primarily of material on
Irish, Scottish, and Welsh church history, history, folk-lore,
sports, economic history, politics, law, and music, and on
Catholic philosophy, Catholic and Anglican theology and church
history, and English Reformation history. The O'Toole collection
consisted of about 2,500 bound volumes (plus unbound periodicals)
focusing on the Irish, Scottish Gaelic, and Welsh languages and
literatures published in the Celtic languages in the period 1875-
1945.

A final source of Special Collections material came to the
College in 1918-1919 from the estates of Archbishop John Ireland
(1838-1918) and Fr. William Etzel (1860-1919, the College's first
Librarian 1912-1918). Etzel, who was educated in France,
collected a small group of fine 18th and 19th century French
editions of journals, letters, and memoirs of the French court
and aristocracy from the period 1500-1815, which came to the
College Library after his death. Archbishop Ireland was also
educated in France and a number of his French books (which again
included many historical memoirs) found their way to the College
library shortly after his death in 1918. Ireland had inherited
some books from one of his predecessors as ordinary of St. Paul,
Bishop Joseph Cretin, another French-educated prelate. These
books were a part of the Ireland collection which was
incorporated into the College library.

146

College of St. Thomas
St. Paul, Minnesota

The Department also houses a small number of literary
autographs and first editions of Catholic authors (e.g. Belloc,
Knox, Greene, Waugh, Fitzgerald) acquired through a number of
individual donations. The James Kellen donation of Belloc books
in 1984 was the most substantive source of the Department's
"Catholic" literary works.

The primary constituencies served by the Department are the
College community (faculty, staff, students, alumni), the Celtic-
Studies scholarly community, members of local ethnic and national
societies (e.g. the St. Andrew's Society, the St. David's
Society, the Irish Section of the Minnesota Genealogical
Society), and local family historians.

II. COLLECTING AREAS.

A. GENERAL WORKS. No attempt to actively collect in this area.

B. PHILOSOPHY. Classics of Catholic philosophy in pre-1820
    editions.

-- PSYCHOLOGY. No attempt to actively collect in this area.

-- RELIGION. Classics of Catholic and Anglican theology and
    spirituality in pre-1820 editions. Books on Celtic and
    English church history, and Catholic-Anglican relations in
    pre-1946 editions.

C. AUXILIARY SCIENCES OF HISTORY. Nearly anything relating to
    the Celtic nations, excluding Brittany, particularly
    biographical directories and family histories in pre-1946
    editions. Some comtemporary books about genealogical
    research will be housed by the Department.

D. GENERAL AND OLD WORLD HISTORY. Nearly anything relating to
    the major Celtic nations, excluding Brittany, in pre-1946
    editions, particularly local (regional, county, barony,
    parish, or village) histories. Journals, letters, and
    memoirs of the French court and aristocracy covering the
    period 1500-1815 in pre-1919 editions.

E. NEW WORLD HISTORY. Immigration lists from Celtic nations.
    No extensive national coverage of the Celtic peoples in the
    new world will be attempted.
F. LOCAL HISTORY. Items on the Celtic peoples in Minnesota,
    Wisconsin, and Iowa. Pre-1900 Minnesota and Twin City
    historical works.

G. GEOGRAPHY. Representative books, maps, and atlases of the
    Celtic nations, excluding Brittany, in pre-1946 editions.

-- ANTHROPOLOGY. No attempt to actively collect in this area.

-- FOLK-LORE AND CUSTOMS. Nearly anything on the folk-lore of
    the Celtic nations, excluding Brittany. Texts of national
    folk cycles, sagas, and tales plus commentary on this
    material in pre-1946 editions.

-- SPORTS AND RECREATION. Works on shooting, fox hunting,
    hunting, horse breeding and racing, and fishing in the
    Celtic nations, excluding Brittany, plus works on Celtic
    sports (e.g. shinny, curling, hurling) in pre-1946 editions.

H. STATISTICS. No attempt to actively collect in this area.

-- ECONOMICS. Certain aspects of Celtic economic history,
    notably the Scottish Highland clearances and the 19th
    century Irish land war.

-- TRANSPORTATION AND COMMUNICATION. Irish telephone
    directories.

-- BUSINESS AND FINANCE. No attempt to actively collect in
    this area.

-- SOCIOLOGY. No attempt to actively collect in this area.

J. POLITICAL SCIENCE. Nearly anything on: the history of the
    Irish Free State government (1922-1949), the government of
    Northern Ireland, the 19th century Imperial admisistration
    of Ireland, the pre-Union governments of Ireland and
    Scotland, and the pre-Norman Conquest governmental systems
    of the Celtic peoples, in pre-1946 editions.

K. LAW. Works on the Irish Brehan law system. Transcripts of
    and commentaries on major political trials in the Celtic
    nations, excluding Brittany, particularly treason or
    sedition trials, in pre-1946 editions.

L. EDUCATION. Material on the Irish hedge schools, in pre-1946
    editions.

M. MUSIC. Tunes and lyrics of folk-music of the Celtic
    nations, excluding Brittany, in pre-1946 editions.

College of St. Thomas
St. Paul Minnesota

N. FINE ARTS. No attempt to actively collect in this area.

P. LANGUAGE AND LITERATURE.

-- The Celtic Collection includes a strong collection of
    material on the history and grammar of the Celtic languages,
    particularly Irish, Scottish Gaelic and Welsh. The
    Collection is also strong in literature in the Irish
    language. However, until the library or College staff
    includes someone with a facility in the Celtic languages, no
    active collection will be attempted in these areas.

-- The Celtic Collection includes a small collection of the
    English-language literature of the Celtic nations. Since
    any attempt to be inclusive in thes area would demand a
    substantial collecting effort, and since collections of this
    sort exist elsewhere, no active collecting will be attempted
    in this area.

-- First or autograph editions of prominent English and
    American Catholic authors (e.g. Belloc, Knox, Waugh, Greene,
    Fitzgerald) will be accepted but not actively sought.

Q. MATHEMATICS, PHYSICS, CHEMISTRY, GEOLOGY, BIOLOGY. Pre-1820
    editions of works by Celtic authors will be accepted but not
    actively sought.

R. MEDICINE. Pre-1820 editions of works by Celtic authors will
    be accepted but not actively sought.

S. AGRICULTURE. No attempt to actively collect in this area.

T. TECHNOLOGY. No attempt to actively collect in this area.

U.-V. MILITARY AND NAVAL SCIENCE. No attempt ot actively
       collect in this area.

Z. BIBLIOGRAPHY AND LIBRARY SCIENCE. History of books and
    manuscripts, publishing, and libraries in the Celtic
    nations, excluding Brittany, in pre-1946 editions.

College of St. Thomas
St. Paul, Minnesota

III. CRITERIA FOR EVALUATING FUTURE POTENTIAL DONATIONS IN NEW
     SUBJECT AREAS.

A. The collection of material should be substantial enough and
    will enough focused to provide the basis for scholarly
    research in a subject area.

B. There must be adequate funds available to insure that the
    subject collection can be maintained and developed.

C. There should be some relationship or potential relationship
    between the subject matter of the collection and the
    curriculum of the College.

D. The items of the potential donation, because of physical
    state, age, subject matter, number in print, edition, or
    availability, must be, or potentially must be, difficult
    items to acquire or replace.

Fairfield University
Fairfield, Connecticut

Archives Acquisitions Guidelines

University Materials

A. Materials for Archival Inclusion:

1. Minutes and records of the Board of Trustees

2. Minutes and records of the several faculties, the general faculty, and faculty committees

3. Minutes and records of administrative and university-wide committees, regular, special, and ad hoc

4. Presidential correspondence

5. Official reports, periodic and special (including accreditation reports, auditors' reports)

6. Catalogs and bulletins, general and special; recruiting materials

7. Special publications (e.g. press releases, calendars, posters, notices of special events)

8. Student publications (e.g. newspapers, yearbooks)

9. Records of student organizations and activities

10. Non-University publications

    a. Newspaper clippings and scrapbooks (on a selective basis)

    b. Pamphlets and books dealing wholly or in part with Fairfield University

11. Pictorial materials, including photographs, campus plans, building plans, rendering of campus buildings. (Individuals in photographs to be identified if possible before transfer to archives)

12. Association materials

    a. Theses

    b. Publications with the Fairfield University imprint

    c. Publications of the Alumni Association

Archives Acquisitions Guidelines

12 continued

    d. Records of organizations associated with the University
        (advisory committees, friends groups, etc.)

13. Appropriate material from interested alumni

14. Jesuit material only if directly related to the founding and
      operation of the University (but including New England Province Catalogs)

15. Monographic publications by faculty

B. Materials to be excluded unless their substance relates to the University:

1. Jesuitica, except as noted above, (Items such as the Jesuit yearbooks,
    Archivum Historicum Societatis Iesu, etc. are included in the Library's
    general collection)

2. Faculty publications other than monographs

3. Publications by alumni

4. Regalia

5. Personal memorabilia

6. Material related to community and other non-University organizations
    in which University personnel have participated

7. Works of art

Detailed Prep Guidelines to be established; Prep Yearbooks and catalogs
are wanted.

Fairfield University
Fairfield, Connecticut
Archival Acquisitions Guidelines
Fairfield Prep Materials

1. Minutes and records of administrative, faculty and departmental committees.

2. Correspondence of the principal.

3. Official reports, periodic and special.

4. Catalogs, bulletins, and recruiting materials.

5. Student publications (including yearbooks and newspapers).

6. Newspaper clippings, building plans, and photographs.

7. Records of student alumni, organizations, friends, and kindred organizations.

8. Monographic publications by faculty.

Exclude

1. Jesuitica, unless directly relating to founding or operation of Fairfield
    Prep.

2. Faculty publications other than monographs.

3. Regalia

4. Personal memoralibilia.

5. Material related to non-Prep organizations in which Prep personnel have
    participated.

6. Works of art.

POLICIES FOR SPECIAL FORMATS

Albion College
Albion, Michigan

- - D R A F T - -

Library Policy for the Selection of Computer Software

December 10, 1986

File name: Soft

The library is committed to providing access to all
types of information regardless of format. Curriculum and
research-related computer software* that satisfies the needs
of the library's primary clientele, i.e., students, faculty,
and staff, falls within the scope of our collection development policy. However, the high cost of these materials
relative to other formats requires that the selection process
be a particularly thoughtful one. The following guidelines
are intended to insure that:

    a.) the library acquire computer software appropri-
        ate to the needs of our primary clientele,
    b.) the purchase of computer software and all
        non-print media not be made at the expense of
        the print collections, and
    c.) the purchase of software be done in an equi-
        table fashion.

GUIDELINES FOR SELECTORS:

    1.) Subject scope: Evaluate textual and numeric data
bases in relationship to the instructional and research interests of our user community.

    2.) User need: Examine the information needs of our
users to determine if primary data is needed in this format.

    3.) Uniqueness of data: Determine if the data is al-
ready available in the library in another format.

    4.) Authority of data: Examine the data to assess au-
thoritativeness and completeness. For example, data repre-
senting research in progress that will undergo significant
change should be considered carefully before purchase.

    5.) Confidentiality of data: Determine if textual and
numeric data files include proprietary or restricted information or have suppressed information to insure confidential-
ity. In this case, their use to the library's primary clientele may be limited.

    6.) Physical format: Make a studied choice between the
formats in which the data may be available, e.g., floppy
disk, disk pack, optical disk, or print.

Albion College
Albion, Michigan

7.) **Documentation, consulting and instructional support**: Assure that documentation adequate for effective use is available and acquired for all software purchased. Some files and programs may require staff assistance to patrons. Consideration must be given to who will provide this assistance.

8.) **Extent of utilization**: Determine the extent to which the material is expected to be used as judged by expressed interest, number of classes to which it is appropriate, and the quality of content and technical quality.

9.) **Duplication and backup**: Consider the need for duplication of heavily used items and the replacement of damaged items. Consider also whether a back-up copy is supplied or whether we are allowed to make one.

ACQUISITION POLICY:

1.) Computer software purchased from library funds must support Albion College curricular or research needs. The library does not purchase software:

    a.) intended for the use of a single individual;
    b.) that, under contractual agreements, can only be used by one person; or
    c.) that is unlikely to be of broad interest, e.g., files consisting of special purpose agregations of data for a single user.

2.) The library purchases software only when the magnitude of the research project or teaching need warrants the expenditure.

3.) The library does not purchase from materials accounts software intended strictly for the manipulation of data, e.g., word processing, spread sheet, and data base management programs.

4.) The library does not purchase recreational software. Only games with sufficient educational or instructional value for use in course work will be purchased.

5.) The total expended on non-print materials, including computer software, shall not exceed 10% of the library's materials budget. No more than 10% of any individual line item in the library's materials budget, i.e., departmental book allocations and library discretionary accounts, may be spent on non-print materials, including software. When a department has spent 10% of its allocation on non-print materials, further requests may be considered for purchase from library accounts.

6.) All software purchased from the library's materials budgets shall:

Albion College
Albion, Michigan

a.) become the property of the library,
b.) be cataloged as part of the library's collections,
c.) be housed in the library,
d.) run on hardware available in the library.

7.) Final authority to purchase software from the library's materials budget, i.e., departmental allocations and library accounts, rests with the library.

CIRCULATION OF SOFTWARE:

Computer software cataloged for the library's collections and intended for the use of the library's clientele may be:
a.) used in the library, or
b.) charged out for a period not to exceed one week.

Documentation may not be circulated independently of the software.

- -

*Software is defined as any program used to operate a computer or manipulate stored, coded data; and as machine-readable data files (MRDF), i.e., any collection of textual or numeric data that can be accessed and or manipulated by computer.

University of Scranton
Scranton, Pennsylvania

The following types of materials will be included in Alumni
Memorial Library for the ---------------collection.

monographs	government documents
serials	research and development reports
microforms	technical reports
newspapers	college catalogs
maps	atlases
pamphlets	proceedings of various groups
newsletters	proceedings of various organizations
reprints, preprints	conference proceedings
student theses	specifications and standards
bibliographies	filmographies
indexes	discographies
abstracts	encyclopedias
directories	dictionaries
handbooks	grammars
sourcebooks	citators
guidebooks	digests
court decisions	regulations and rulings
legislative materials	constitutional materials
slides	sound recordings
filmstrips	transparencies
motion pictures	audio-visual materials
videotapes	curriculum guides

Except for materials in the achival collection, the following
materials will be excluded from the -------------
collection:

dissertations	charts
textbooks	special studies
gazettes	letters and private papers
personal journals	lecture notes
scrolls	field notes
standard tests	newspaper clippings
posters	scrapbooks
albums	programs
paintings	scene designs
sculpture	costume designs
models	artifacts
specimens	photographs
pictures	portfolios
signatures	medical instruments
patents	iconographic materials
drawings	educational games

University of Scranton
Scranton, Pennsylvania

(The following materials should by added to either the included
or excluded category, depending on the subject being profiled)

foreign documents
international documents
corporate reports
technical reports
museum catalogs
treatises, compendiums
manuscripts, typescripts
facsimiles of manuscripts
lab manuals
catalogs of instruments
computer programs
magnetic diskettes
private and company files
equipment manuals
devotional religious books

MISCELLANEOUS POLICIES

Clarion State College
Clarion, Pennsylvania

University Libraries

Policy and Procedure Memorandum 1.4.2 rev.

Department: University Libraries

Authorization: Materials Selection Committee

Distribution: Library Faculty

Subject: Collection Management:
                       Withdrawal Policy

Date: March 12, 1986

The Libraries' commitment to the mission statement of the
institution requires maintaining a library collection of the
highest quality. The policy for removal of materials from the
general collections is described in this document. The
maintenance of an ongoing withdrawal policy as time and schedules
permit is of great importance in preserving the quality desired
in the library's collections. Withdrawal takes three forms:
withdrawal for discard, withdrawal for storage, and withdrawal
for transfer. Lost materials are treated in a separate policy.

The Collections Librarian is responsible for the supervision and
maintenance of the general collections, the arrangement of
shelving, and the general review of materials contained within
the general collections. The Collections Librarian will usually
initiate all withdrawal actions, based on space requirements, in
response to requests, and will coordinate that effort with the
subject specialist. Prior announcement of classifications
subject to withdrawal will be made by memorandum to all
librarians. Materials subject to withdrawal may include obsolete
items; materials which have not circulated for a specified period
of time unless a standard author or title is involved; out of
date topical items; superseded editions; isolated serials; broken
sets; vanity publications; unused journal backfiles; historical
materials in subject fields which have little relationship to
current interest; little used sets unless representative of
standard authors; textbooks and materials not included in current
selection policies and otherwise of doubtful value.

Preliminary determination of the category into which a withdrawn
item will fall (discard, storage, or transfer) is made by the
subject specialist, who works closely with the Collections
Librarian in the withdrawal process. It is the responsibility of
the Collections librarian to notify the subject specialist of the
need for withdrawal actions in the specialist's area of the
collection, in a timely manner that enables the specialist to
fulfill his responsibilities in the withdrawal process.

Clarion State College
Clarion, Pennsylvania

Policy and Procedure Memorandum 1.4.2 rev.

It is the responsibility of the subject specialist to review all
items pulled for withdrawal within a specified period of time,
and determine into which withdrawal category they fall (discard,
storage, or transfer). It is also the responsibility of the
subject specialist to notify all librarians and the teaching
faculty who will be affected by such withdrawal actions, in a
timely manner that enables them to review the items under
consideration.

Librarians other then the subject specialist who would like to
review or offer their opinions regarding items under
consideration for withdrawal should speak directly to the subject
specialist.

Withdrawal for Discard:

The establishment of guidelines and criteria for discarding
material in specific areas is the joint responsibility of the
subject specialist and the Collections Librarian. A written
statement of these criteria, using the guidelines set forth in
the American Library Association's Guidelines for Collection
Development (1979) should be developed by the subject specialist,
in consultation with the teaching faculty involved and the
Collections Librarian.

Withdrawal for Storage:

When a book's value to the general collection is in question, the
subject specialist may use the option of withdrawing the book to
storage. The withdrawal to storage option may also be useful for
resolving problems that may arise when teaching faculty and other
librarians review the materials considered for withdrawal.

Books withdrawn to storage are held there for a retention period
of 2 years. During this time, items are subject to recall, and
if recalled, are returned to the general collection stacks.
After the two-year retention period has expired, the subject
specialist and the Collections Librarian will decide whether to
return the material to the collection or discard it.

This option is designed for use on an item-by-item basis as noted
above, not as an overflow area for crowded sections of the
general collection.

Withdrawal for Transfer:

After appropriate review by the Collections Librarian and the
subject specialist, certain items may be withdrawn from the
general collections for transfer to other institutions. This can
be as a result of a cooperative agreement wherein another state

Clarion State College
Clarion, Pennsylvania

Policy and Procedure Memorandum 1.4.2 rev.

academic library has agreed to maintain a particular backfile and
current subscription of an expensive journal for possible
interlibrary loan by libraries or others within the Pennsylvania
system.   This effort is coordinated with the Catalog Department.
Such transfers are also subject to regional agreements, exchange
with other institutions, and similar methods whereby libraries
reinforce their collection policies or engage in resource
sharing.

Tri-College University

TRI-COLLEGE LIBRARY ACQUISITION POLICY
November, 1977

Purpose

The Tri-College University is a consortium consisting of Concordia College, Moorhead State University, and North Dakota State University. Its purpose is to provide a broader range of programs, more extensive facilities, and a greater depth of resources for the students and faculties of the three institutions than would otherwise be available. The purpose of this policy is to serve as a guide to cooperation in collection development for the three institution libraries.

Philosophy

TCU Librarians recognize that cooperation in collection development will tend to result in an interdependence of the individual collections. However, in response to the dual economic realities of increasing materials costs and tightening budgets; in accord with accrediting agencies' recognition of "accessibility" as a factor in collection building; and in accord with the continuing viability of the Tri-College University Consortium, the libraries agree to implement this program under the following provisions:

A. The implementation of this policy shall not substitute for development of adequate individual collections based on the obligation to support curricular and user needs.

B. Cooperation shall be implemented through the TCUL Acquisitions Task Force, who are delegated the primary responsibility for collection development.

C. Task Force decisions shall be guided by the following considerations:
1. The curriculum and user needs of the individual institutions.
2. The selection and acquisition policies of the individual libraries.
3. The existing identified strengths of the individual library collections.
4. The cost, demand for, and accessibility to an individual item.

D. Within these guidelines, TCU Libraries may:
1. Compare selections to be purchased for the purpose of reducing unnecessary duplication.
2. Combine existing holdings of items (such as incomplete sets).
3. Jointly purchase specific items.

168

Tri-College University

E. This Tri-College Library Acquisition Policy shall receive at least an annual review by the TCU Acquisitions Task Force. This review shall take into consideration the curricular growth and development at each of the Tri-College University institutions.

Definitions for Levels of Collection Density and Collection Intensity

"The terms defined below are designed for use in identifying both the extent of existing collections in given subject fields (collection density) and the extent of current collecting activity in the field (collection intensity).

A. Comprehensive level. A collection in which a library endeavors, so far as is reasonably possible, to include all significant works of recorded knowledge (publications, manuscripts, other forms), in all applicable languages, for a necessarily defined and limited field. This level of collection intensity is that which maintains a 'special collection'; the aim, if not the achievement, is exhaustiveness.

B. Research level. A collection which includes the major source materials required for dissertations and independent research, including materials containing research reporting, new findings, scientific experimental results, and other information useful to researchers. It also includes all important reference works and a wide selection of specialized monographs, as well as a very extensive collection of journals and major indexing and abstracting services in the field.

C. 1. Advanced study level. A collection which is adequate to support the course work of advanced undergraduate and master's degree programs, or sustained independent study; that is, which is adequate to maintain knowledge of a subject required for limited or generalized purposes, of less than research intensity. It includes a wide range of basic monographs both current and retrospective, complete collections of the works of more important writers, selections from the works of secondary writers, a selection of representative journals, and the reference tools and fundamental bibliographical apparatus pertaining to the subject.

2. Initial study level. A collection which is adequate to support undergraduate courses. It includes a judicious selection from

> currently published basic monographs (as are represented by
> Choice selections) supported by seminal retrospective monographs
> (as are represented by Books for College Libraries); a broad
> selection of works of more important writers; a selection of the
> most significant works of secondary writers; a selection of the
> major review journals; and current editions of the most
> significant reference tools and bibliographies pertaining to the
> subject.[1]

D. Basic level. A highly selective collection which serves to introduce
and define the subject and to indicate the varieties of information
available elsewhere. It includes major dictionaries and encyclopedias,
selected editions of important works, historical surveys, important
bibliographies, and a few major periodicals in the field.

E. Minimal level. A subject area which is out of scope for the library's
collections, and in which few selections are made beyond very basic
reference tools.

The definitions are proposed to describe a range of diversity of titles and
forms of material; they do not address the question of availability of multiple
copies of the same title."[2]

---

[1] American Library Association. Collection Development Committee. Guidelines
for Collection Development. David L. Perkins, Editor. Chicago: A.L.A., c1979,
p. 4.

[2] American Library Association. Resources and Technical Services Division.
Resources Section. Collection Development Committee. "Guidelines for the
formulation of collection development policies." Library Resources and Technical
Services, 21:42-3, Winter, 1977.

Tri-College University
TCU ACQUISITIONS TASK FORCE POLICY CHANGES

At the present time libraries face an extreme reduction in buying power caused by three factors: budgetary constraints, spiraling inflation causing an increase in prices for materials, and a continuing flow of new publications. We recognize the ideal situation is for each library to continue its current policy of supplying nearly all the materials for its curriculum. However, the Tri-College Acquisitions Task Force is finding it increasingly difficult to attain this ideal and, for that reason, it has proposed and we are recommending the changes which follow the discussion of current policy.

Current Policy

Members of the Acquisitions Task Force select from Choice (a monthly book-selection journal published by the Association of College and Research Libraries) to support the curriculum served by their individual libraries. Duplication is made rather generously with the exception of very expensive books or of materials which, in our judgement, will not be heavily used. The philosophy has been that each library is responsible for the materials necessary to support the courses taught on its own campus, such support being approximately 85-90% of materials needed. This philosophy has been the basis for the generous duplicating of materials.

We have also selected materials keeping in mind that we are building a broad basic collection which we feel is a necessity for any quality academic library. This material may be of a general nature including basic sources in each field, materials at an undergraduate level, materials which cross departmental lines, and standard and definitive works.

This policy requires duplication of materials in areas of study taught on all of the campuses, chiefly in most of the liberal arts. However, since the strength of the programs varies from campus to campus, each librarian attempts to correlate the intensity of collecting with the strength of the programs, bearing in mind the amount of material published in each area.

Finally, according to the Tri-College Acquisitions Policy, each of the three libraries has assumed the responsibility for developing an in-depth collection in certain subject areas: NDSU--the sciences and technology, architecture, home economics, access tools such as indices and bibliographies; MSU--education, business, music, law; CONCORDIA--religion, philosophy, classics, Jewish studies, East Africa studies.

The following recommended changes apply to circulating materials only, as we recognize that each campus library must maintain a core reference collection appropriate to its needs.

Purchase

In general, limit to one copy the purchase of items specified for upper undergraduate, graduate, or professional levels as indicated by Choice or other reviewing tools.

Discontinue purchase of all out-of-print materials except in situations justified for special purposes.

Tri-College University

Purchase foreign language materials only for the study of languages except in situations justified for special purposes.

Purchase the least expensive format when there is a choice.

Eliminate duplication of major sets such as complete works, letters, variorum editions, papers, annual reviews, progress in, methods in, etc.

Selection

Emphasize to the faculty the desirability of selecting materials from critical reviews or examination of materials, rather than selecting from publishers' advertisements or catalogs.

Search and Verification

Work toward a Tri-College on-line database for on-order files and items ready to order to enable each acquisitions department to compare all local selections with those made on the other campuses. This will provide, reasonably, the capability of reducing duplication to a minimal level.

Implications of Policy Changes

The proposals listed under Purchase will provide more unique titles in the Tri-College University but fewer duplicated titles on individual campuses.

The above fact may well increase intercampus borrowing and necessitate changes in the shuttle service.

Implementation of policy changes suggested may necessitate changes in circulation policies, especially long-term loans.

Selection implies that the acquisition or library liaison personnel will need to actively encourage the faculty to understand the importance of selecting from reviews.

Access to a database of TCU order files is essential for optimum coopera- tion and resource sharing.

Optimum cooperation may result in increased communication among tri-campus academic departments.

Implementation of policy changes suggested would alter the individual libraries' collections beyond the point where losses can be recouped.

Implementation of policy changes affirms the establishment of a philosophy that supports collection development with a view toward unified strength rather than three single, balanced, and duplicated collections.

Tri-College Library Directors, June 3, 1982

Approved by Tri-College Commissioners, September 27, 1982

172

Tri-College University

<u>LEVELS OF COLLECTING AT THE THREE LIBRARIES</u>

Key to Symbols: A = Comprehensive
                 B = Research
                 C1 = Advanced study level for advanced undergraduates and
                      Master's programs
                 C2 = Initial study level for undergraduate courses
                 D = Basic level
                 E = Minimal

		CC	MSU	NDSU
A --	**GENERAL WORKS**			
AC	Collections. Series			D
AE	Encyclopedias (General)	C2	C1	C1
AG	General Reference Works	C2	C1	C1
AI	Indexes	C2	C1	B
AM	Museums	C2	C2	D
AN	Newspapers	C2	C1	D
AP	Periodicals (General)	C2	C2	C1
AS	Societies. Academies	C2		C1
AY	Yearbooks (General)	C2	C2	C2
AZ	General History of Knowledge			
	and Learning	C2	C2	C2
*B --	**PHILOSOPHY-RELIGION**			
B	Collections	C1	C1	D
BC	Logic	C2	C1	C2
BD	Metaphysics	C1	C1	D
BF	Psychology	C1	C1	C1
BH	Esthetics	D	C1	D
BJ	Ethics. Religion, Theology	C1	C2	C2
BL	Religions	C1	C1	D
BM	Judaism	C1	D	D
BP	Christianity	C1	D	D
BR	Generalities. Church History	C1	D	C1
	(Lutheran)	C1		
BS	Bible and Exegesis	C1	D	C2
BT	Doctrinal Theology	C1	E	E
BV	Practical Theology	C1	E	D
BX	Special Sects	C1	D	D
C --	**HISTORY-AUXILIARY SCIENCES**			
CB	History of Civilization	C2	C1	C2
CC	Antiquities (General)	C2	C1	E
CD	Archives	E	D	C2
CE	Chronology	C2	E	D

* The classification B at Concordia includes an in-depth collection of
  Kierkegaard, Luther, and various aspects of death.

Tri-College University		CC	MSU	NDSU
CJ	Numismatics. Coins	E	E	E
CN	Epigraphy. Inscriptions	D	D	E
CR	Heraldry	D	D	D
CS	Genealogy	C2	E	E
CT	Biography	C2	C1	C2

D -- HISTORY AND TOPOGRAPHY (except America)

D	General History	C2	C1	C2
DA	Great Britain	C2	C1	C1
DB	Austria - Hungary	C2	C2	C2
DC	France	C2	C1	C1
DD	Germany	C2	C1	C1
DE	Classical Antiquity	C2	C1	E
DF	Greece	C2	C1	D
DG	Italy	D	C1	D
DH-				
DJ	Netherlands	D	C2	D
DK	Russia	C2	C1	C1
DL	Scandinavia	C2	C1	D
DP	Spain and Portugal	D	C1	D
DQ	Switzerland	D	C2	D
DR	Turkey, Balkan States	D	D	E
DS	Asia	C2	C2	C2
DT	Africa	C2	C1	D
DU	Australia, Oceania	D	D	D
DX	Gypsies	E	E	E

E -- AMERICA AND UNITED STATES

11	America (General)	C1	C1	C2
31	North America (General)	C1	C1	C1
51	Indians	C1	C1	C1
101	Discovery of America	C2	C1	C2
151	United States. General			C2
169	History U.S. - Civilization	C1	C1	C1
185	Negroes	C1	C1	C2
186	Colonial Period	C2	C1	C1
201	Revolution	C2	C1	C1
351	War of 1812	C2	C1	D
401	War with Mexico	C2	C1	D
441	Slavery	C1	C1	C2
458	Civil War	C2	C1	C1
482	Confederate States	C2	C1	C2
714	War with Spain	C2	C1	C2

F -- UNITED STATES (Local) AND AMERICA
    (except the U.S.)

1	United States (Local)	D2	D	D
631-				
645	Red River Valley Regional Studies	C2		B
1001	British North America	D	C2	C2

Tri-College University

		CC	MSU	NDSU
1201	Mexico	D	D	D
1401	Latin America (General)	D	C2	E
1421	Central America	D	D	E
1601	West Indies	D	D	E
2201	South America (General)	D	C2	E
2251	Columbia	D	D	E
2301	Venezuela	D	D	E
2351	Guiana	D	D	E
2501	Brazil	D	D	E
2661	Paraguay	D	D	E
2701	Uruguay	D	D	E
2801	Argentine Republic	D	D	E
3051	Chile	D	D	E
3301	Bolivia	D	D	E
3401	Peru	D	D	E
3701	Ecuador	D	D	E

G -- GEOGRAPHY-ANTHROPOLOGY

		CC	MSU	NDSU
G	Geography (General)	D	C2	C2
GA	Mathematical Geography	D	D	D
GB	Physical Geography	D	C2	C2
GC	Oceanology	D	D	D
GF	Anthropogeography	D	D	C2
GN	Anthropology	D	C1	C1
GR	Folklore	D	C2	D
GT	Manners and Customs	D	D	D
GV	Sports and Amusements	C2	C1	C1

H -- SOCIAL SCIENCES

		CC	MSU	NDSU
H	Social Science (General)	D	C1	C2
HA	Statistics	D	C1	C1
HB	Economic Theory	C2	C1	C1
HC	Economic History	C2	C1	C2
HD	Economic History: Agriculture	D	D	C1
HE	Transportation	D	C2	C2
HF	Commerce	D	C1	C1
HG	Finance	C2	C1	C1
HJ	Public Finance	C2	C1	C2
HM	Sociology	C2	C1	C1
HN	Social History	C2	C1	C2
HQ	Family (Women)	C2	C1	C2
HS	Associations	D	D	E
HT	Communities	D	C1	C2
HV	Social Pathology	C2	D	C1
HX	Socialism, Communism	C2	C1	C2

J -- POLITICAL SCIENCE

		CC	MSU	NDSU
J	Documents	D	C1	D
JA	General Works	C2	C1	C1

Tri-College University		CC	MSU	NDSU
JC	Political Science. Constitutional History	C2	C1	C1
JF	General Works	C2	C1	C2
JK	United States	C2	C1	C1
JL	British America. Latin America	D	D	D
JN	Europe	D	D	D
JQ	Asia, Africa, Australia	D	D	E
JS	Local Government	D	C1	C2
JV	Colonies	D	D	E
JX	International Law	D	C1	D

K -- LAW

K	General	C2	C1	D
KBB	Ancient Law	E	E	E
KBD	Roman Law. Theocratic Legal Systems. Christian	E	E	E
KBL	Islamic	E	E	E
KBM	Jewish	E	E	E
KD	United Kingdom. Anglo-American Law	E	E	E
KE	Canada	E	E	E
KF	United States	C2	C1	C1
KG	Latin America (includes Mexico, Central and South America)	E	E	E
KJ	Europe (Western)	E	E	E
KK	Europe (Central)	E	E	E
KL	Europe (Southeastern)	E	E	E
KLP	Europe (Northern)	E	E	E
KM	Soviet Union	E	E	E
KP	Asia (Southwestern Asia. The Near East)	E	E	E
KPK	Asia (Southern)	E	E	E
KQ	Asia (Southeastern. The Far East)	E	E	E
KR	Africa	E	E	E
KT	Australia. New Zealand. Oceania. Antarctica.	E	E	E

L -- EDUCATION

L	General Works	C2	C1	C2
LA	History of Education	D	C1	C2
LB	Theory and Practice	C2	C1	C1
LC	Special Forms	D	C1	D
LD	United States	D	C1	C1
LE	Other American	E	D	E
LF	Europe	E	D	E
LG	Asia, Africa	E	D	E
LH	University, College	D	C2	D
LJ	Fraternities	E	E	E
LT	Textbooks (K-12)	C2	C1	E

Tri-College University

		CC	MSU	NDSU
M -- MUSIC				
M	Music			
5	One Instrument		C1	C2
	(Hymns)	C2		
177	Several Instruments	D	C1	C2
1000	Orchestra	D	C1	D
1450	Dance Music	D	C1	E
1495	Vocal Music	D	C1	C1
ML	Literature of Music			
48	Librettos	D	C1	C2
159	History and Criticism	C2	C1	C1
3800	Philosophy, Physics, Psychology,			
	Esthetics	D	C1	E
MT	Musical Instruction	C2	C1	C1
N -- FINE ARTS				
N	General	C2	C1	C2
NA	Architecture	D	D	C1
NB	Sculpture	C2	C1	E
NC	Graphic Arts	C2	C1	C2
ND	Painting	C2	C1	C2
NE	Engraving	D	C1	E
NK	Art Applied to Industry	D	D	E
P -- LANGUAGE AND LITERATURE				
P	Philology and Linguistics	C2	C1	C2
PA	Classical Languages	C2	E	·E
PB	Celtic Languages	E	E	E
PC	Romance Languages	C2	C2	C2
PD	Germanic Languages	C2	C2	E
PE	English, Middle English, Anglo-Saxon	C2	C2	C2
PF	Dutch	E	E	E
PG	Slavic	E	E	E
PH	Finnish, Basque	E	E	E
PJ	Egyptian. Semitic	E	E	E
PN	Literary History	C2	C1	C1
PQ	Romance Literatures	C2	D	C1
PR	English Literature	C1	C1	C1
PS	American Literature	C1	C1	C1
PT	Teutonic Literature	C2	D	D
	Children's Literature	D	C1	E
Q -- SCIENCE				
Q	Science (General)	C2	C1	C1
QA	Mathematics	C2	C1	C1
QB	Astronomy	D	C2	C2
QC	Physics	D	C1	B
QD	Chemistry	D	C1	B
QE	Geology	D	C2	C2

Tri-College University		CC	MSU	NDSU
QH	Natural History	D	C1	C1
QK	Botany	C2	C1	B
QL	Zoology	C2	C1	B
QM	Human Anatomy	C2	C1	C1
QP	Physiology	C2	C1	C1
QR	Bacteriology	D	C1	B

R -- MEDICINE

R	Medicine (General	D	D	D
RA	Hygiene	D	C1	C2
RB	Pathology		E	E
RC	Practice	E	E	E
RD	Surgery	E	E	E
RE	Ophthalmology	E	E	E
RF	Otology	E	E	E
RG	Gynecology	E	E	E
RJ	Pediatrics	E	E	E
RK	Dentistry	E	E	E
RL	Dermatology	E	E	E
RM	Therapeutics	E	E	E
RS	Pharmacy	E	E	B
RT	Nursing	e1	C1	C1
RX	Homeopathy	E	E	E
RZ	Miscellaneous	E	E	E

S -- AGRICULTURE

S	Agriculture (General)	E	E	B
SB	Plant Culture	E	E	B
SD	Forestry	E	E	C2
SF	Animal Culture	E	E	B
SH	Fish Culture	E	E	B
SK	Hunting Sports	E	E	E

T -- TECHNOLOGY

T	Technology (General	D	D	C1
TA	Engineering (General). Civil Engineering	E	D	B
TC	Hydraulic Engineering	E	D	C1
TD	Sanitary Engineering	E	D	C1
TE	Roads	E	D	C1
TF	Railroad Engineering	E	D	D
TG	Bridges and Roofs	E	D	C1
TH	Building Construction	E	D	C1
TJ	Mechanical Engineering	E	D	B
TK	Electrical Engineering	E	D	B
TL	Motor Vehicles. Aeronautics	E	C2	C1
TN	Mineral Industries	E	D	D
TP	Chemical Technology	D	D	B

Tri-College University		CC	MSU	NDSU
TR	Photography	D	C1	D
TS	Manufactures	E	D	D
TT	Trades	E	D	D
TX	Domestic Science	C2	D	C1

U -- MILITARY SCIENCE

		CC	MSU	NDSU
U	Military Science (General)	E	E	C2
UA	Armies	E	E	D
UB	Administration	E	E	C2
UC	Maintenance	E	E	D
UD	Infantry	E	E	C2
UE	Cavalry	E	E	E
UF	Artillery	E	E	D
UG	Military Engineering	E	E	D
UH	Other Services	E	E	E

V -- NAVAL SCIENCE

		CC	MSU	NDSU
V	Naval Science (General)	E	E	D
VA	Navies	E	E	E
VB	Administration	E	E	E
VC	Maintenance	E	E	E
VD	Seamen	E	E	E
VE	Marines	E	E	E
VF	Naval Ordinance	E	E	E
VG	Other Services	E	E	E
VK	Navigation	E	E	E
VM	Shipbuilding	E	E	E

Z -- BIBLIOGRAPHY AND LIBRARY SCIENCE

		CC	MSU	NDSU
4	History of Books	D	D	D
40	Writing	D	E	E
116	Book Industries	D	D	D
551	Copyright	C2	C2	D
665	Libraries and Library Science	C2	C2	C2
998	Book Prices	E	E	E
1001	Bibliography	C1	C1	B

Revised January 12, 1983

University of the South
Sewanee, Tennessee

CITIZEN'S REQUEST FOR RECONSIDERATION OF LIBRARY MATERIAL

Author: _____ ____Hardcover ____Paperback____Other

Title: _____

Publisher (If known): _____

Telephone: _____ Address: _____

City: _____ Zip Code: _____

Complainant represents:

    ____himself

    ____(Name organization) _____

    ____(Identify other group) _____

(If objection is to material other than a book, change wording of the following questions so that they apply).

1.   To what in the book do you object? Use back of this page if more space is needed for comments. (Please be specific; cite pages.)

    _____

    _____

    _____

    _____

2.   What do you feel might be the result of reading this book?

    _____

    _____

    _____

    _____

3.   For what age group would you recommend this book? _____

    _____

4.   Is there anything good about the book? _____

    _____

University of the South
Sewanee, Tennessee

Citizen's Request for Reconsideration of Library Material

5. Did you read the entire book? _____ What parts? _____

_____

6. Are you aware of the judgment of this book by literary critics?

_____ yes _____ no

7. What do you believe is the theme of this book? _____

_____

_____

_____

_____

8. What would you like the library to do about this book?

_____Withdraw it from the library.

_____Send it back to the staff selection official for
         re-evaluation.

9. In its place, what book of equal literary quality would you
   recommend that would adequately convey a picture and perspective of the subject treated?

_____

_____

_____